MUSIC MAVENS

15

WOMEN OF NOTE IN THE INDUSTRY

ASHLEY WALKER AND
MAUREEN CHARLES

CHICAGO
REVIEW
PRESS

T0182642

For music educators and choir directors everywhere,
those who taught us and those who teach others,
thank you for the music.

It always depends on one teacher.
—Valérie Sainte-Agathe

Contents

Prelude vii

Part I Power to Innovate 1

1 Macy Schmidt: Orchestrating Equity 2
2 Lia Mice: Innovating Inclusion 15
3 Katarina Benzova: Shooting Stars 27

Part II Power to Perform 39

4 Janet Dacal: Hitting Broadway Heights 40
5 Valérie Sainte-Agathe: Stronger Together 52
6 Kaoly Asano: Soul, Spirit, and Sound 65

Part III Power to Compose 77

7 Nami Melumad: Cinematic Scoring 78
8 Joanne Shenandoah: Standing in Power 91
9 Kate Schutt: Presence Not Perfection 101

Part IV Power to Improvise 113

10 Kaila Mullady: Beatboxing Brilliance 114
11 Vân-Ánh Vanessa Võ: Tradition
and Improvisation 126
12 Regina Carter: Call and Response 139

Part V Power to Produce   153
   13 Nova Wav: Songwriting and Producing Duo   154
   14 Maria Elisa Ayerbe: Engineering Latin Sound 168
   15 Sylvia Massy: Adventure Recording   181

Tribute to Sophie Xeon   193

Coda   196

Ovation   198

Playlist   201

Resources   206

Notes   208

Prelude

There are moments that happen on stage, moments of sheer bliss that transcend all.

—Katarina Benzova,
rock photographer and documentarian

Whether you like rock or pop or rap, country or classical or traditional, one thing's certain—music has moved you. Groovy, up-tempo beats get you on your feet. The slow, sweet swing of a lullaby brings on sleep. And a love song deepens affection (when it isn't amplifying heartache).

Music has been doing these things—pumping people up, settling them down, and soothing life's stings—for a long time, ever since our early ancestors circled around firepits with drums and flutes.

Every known human culture—throughout the recorded past and around the modern world—has enjoyed music. Whenever, wherever people come together, music is there too. For most of music's history, people did not think of themselves as either performers or listeners. Instead, music was communal, made and enjoyed by all. But today, many of the songs you hear are recorded in faraway places by artists who shine like distant stars on flat screens. Though you get glimpses of their lives in the media, the sense of distance remains.

In the following chapters, however, *Music Mavens* invites you back into the circle—to sit down next to women of note in the industry.

These artists work across music genres, and they excel in a variety of roles, including composing and songwriting, performing and conducting, as well as audio engineering, producing, and even rock photography.

How did these women defy the odds? We interviewed all of them. And guess what? Few had musical families. No one's best friend owned a studio. Nobody lived next door to a talent scout.

The women in this book are music lovers just like you. Moved by the power of song, they wanted to move others. So, they studied, practiced, and mastered their craft.

Legendary performer Joanne Shenandoah described the drive to make music like this: "You are transported yourself, therefore, you transport others. . . . Once you've done that and you've experienced it and you know it, you want to keep coming back."

Read on to learn how these artists turned their passion into platforms. See how they use their positions to uplift others. Most of all, enjoy the exclusive stories of music mavens who went from mere music lovers to women of note in the industry.

Part I
Power to Innovate

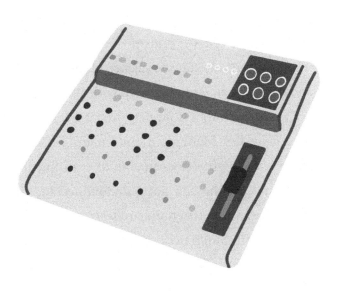

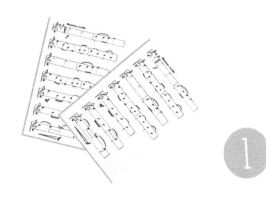

1

Macy Schmidt: Orchestrating Equity

When *Ratatouille: The TikTok Musical* (based on the Disney animated film *Ratatouille*) began streaming on January 1, 2021, online viewers were treated to something rare. Every musician was female, and most were women of color. The Broadway Sinfonietta, the masterful orchestra that accompanied the musical, struck a chord with all who saw and heard it.

The Sinfonietta's founder, Macy Schmidt, watched the show from her Manhattan apartment. Ten years earlier she had entered high school unable to read music. Now, barely out of college, she had not only founded her own orchestra, but she had also written the orchestrations they were playing.

While *Ratatouille* streamed, Macy's social media feeds blew up. People were filled with hope by the sight and sound of the Sinfonietta.

Los Angeles Times theater critic Ashley Lee tweeted, "I have chills from this female, diverse #RatatouilleMusical orchestra."

"I am LIVING for the orchestra, @ratatousical really did that for poc women. Inspiring," tweeted a college student named Tay.

Ratatouille: The TikTok Musical

During the COVID-19 pandemic, writing content for an imagined *Ratatouille* musical captured the imaginations of bored musical theater creatives on TikTok. They posted songs, costume ideas, even a digital, downloadable theater Playbill. In December 2020, Disney greenlighted a one-time benefit performance using those TikTokers' creations. The benefit, streamed in early January 2021, raised $2 million to help unemployed actors.

Macy had started The Broadway Sinfonietta in response to inequities she had witnessed as a woman of color working in musical theater. Now, with *Ratatouille*, her activism had reached 350,000 strangers, and many were reaching back.

How had the 14-year-old who couldn't read music come so far by age 23?

Macy Schmidt was born in Los Angeles to an Egyptian couple who put her up for adoption at birth, then returned to Egypt.

Janet and David Schmidt, a white couple from Texas, quickly adopted baby Macy "not because they had to but because they wanted to." Macy says she "won the parent lottery" with her mom and dad, whose deep parental bond is not a product of biology but of love. "Personality-wise, anyone who knows us would tell you I am 50 percent my father and 50 percent my mother," she says. (Given her experience, it is not surprising that Macy, too, wants to adopt someday.)

The Schmidts remained in Texas until Macy was five. Then the trio moved to Florida, where they lived on the beach, two hours from Disney World, for three idyllic years.

The family returned to Texas when Macy started third grade. There, she attended an elite, private K–12 school, where she received an excellent education but felt suffocated by all the rules. So, eight-year-old Macy often stepped out of line, hoping she would be expelled and returned to Florida freedom. That plan failed.

Fortunately, despite the rigorous environment, academics were never a problem for Macy, who recalls being "very brainy . . . the kid who would win a competition where you see how many digits of pi you can memorize."

Macy also longed to learn piano, so at age 15, she taught herself to play songs from memory by watching videos online and copying what she saw. But she couldn't read music.

Then, in her sophomore year, Macy had an incredible choir teacher named Becky Martin. One day, Becky introduced the class to sight reading, and that first lesson in musical notation changed Macy's life. She was suddenly struck by the relationship between the notes on the page and the sounds she produced. It was "the coolest thing in the world."

Macy became obsessed with music theory and switched to videos that actually taught her to read piano music. For singing, she learned solfége, the use of sol-fa syllables (*do-re-mi-fa-sol-la-ti-do*). She even sang pop songs in the shower replacing the lyrics with solfége. By her senior year, Macy had become so good at reading music that when she auditioned for the Texas All-State Women's Choir, she got a perfect score on her sight singing rounds, earning a coveted spot.

Macy also loved Broadway cast albums, but unlike most kids, she didn't just sing along. Instead, when she got a new album, she would listen to the songs and arrange her own overture (a medley of tunes played by the orchestra before the curtain rises on a musical or opera). Then she listened to the Broadway overture for comparison. Macy had no idea that arranging an overture was an actual job or that it was an advanced skill. She was just having fun.

She was cast in the high school musical her senior year, but she bristled at drama department procedures she considered inequitable. When she spoke up about those injustices, she lost her role in the play. Crushed, she swore off musical theater forever.

Meanwhile, Macy studied opera singing with Cathy Wafford, a "really wonderful" private voice teacher. Heads together, they would pore over a score (the written representation of a musical composition showing the vocal and instrumental parts) discussing its musicality and dynamics (varying levels of volume). Macy loved "the process of marking up a score and learning the theory" (the building blocks of music), but she did not love performing. She didn't find it fulfilling. However, colleges give scholarships for music performance, not theory, so she worked on her vocals and won an opera singing scholarship—and a National Merit Scholarship—to the University of Florida (UF) in Gainesville.

Macy knew she didn't want to be an opera singer, but she trusted she'd find a career path in her beloved Florida, and it didn't take long for that path to appear. At UF she was assigned to work with voice studio professor Dr. Tony Offerle. To her surprise, Tony was a Broadway musical buff who served as music director for UF's theater department. Recognizing her passion for the subject, Tony asked Macy to be his assistant on UF's fall semester musical, and Macy said yes. So much for swearing off musical theater.

What Is a Music Director?

This role oversees all musical aspects of a production—casting performers, hiring the orchestra, rehearsing singers and musicians, and conducting during performances. They must play piano at a high enough level to conduct and play simultaneously.

Macy recalls her first day as Tony's assistant: "I showed up that day, and they had a big orchestra playing the big brass parts, and I just melted. The music of musical theater felt right, and I just slippery-sloped to Broadway headfirst."

Also that first semester, Macy was asked to serve as music director for a student production of *In the Heights*. She had no experience, but she had a great mentor in Tony.

Macy vividly recalls her UF cast doing a video chat with *In the Heights* Broadway cast member Janet Dacal (see chapter 4), who shared her experiences and answered the students' many questions. Macy has never forgotten Janet's generosity.

Those first semester experiences with music directing opened Macy's imagination. By second semester, she'd changed her major to music theory and started applying for summer internships on Broadway. She applied to 100 in all.

During that process, Macy went to New York over spring break, cold e-mailed nearly all 100 internship coordinators and invited them to meet her over a cup of coffee. Cold emailing is sending an email to someone without a prior introduction. A few coordinators actually said yes to a meeting, including Jennifer Tepper, director of programming at Feinstein's/54 Below, a supper club that hosts cabaret shows. Impressed with Macy, Jen offered her an internship.

That summer, Macy met about 16 music directors a week, a different one for every show at Feinstein's. The mere existence of so many music directors gave Macy a reason to believe she might someday join their ranks. And some invited her to assist on other theater projects.

In New York, she met more and more people in more and more roles—music assistants, copyists, orchestrators, arrangers—all with a love for those glorious notes on the page.

Macy wasn't technically qualified to fill those roles yet, but she wanted to be. And doors were beginning to open.

People Who Put the Notes on the Page

A **music assistant** notes all changes to the score during rehearsals—bars cut, parts altered, keys changed, etc. Music assistant is a stepping-stone to copyist.

A **copyist** gets the master score from the orchestrator, formats the music to precise industry standards using notation software, creates pristine sheet music for each instrument, and inserts page turns at the easiest moments—a small detail of great importance.

An **orchestrator** fleshes out the composer's musical sketch assigning notes, chords, rhythms, harmonies, and dynamics (varying levels of loudness between notes or phrases) to the instruments. They don't reinvent the composition; rather, they fulfill the composer's creative vision.

An **arranger** reimagines an existing composition, adapting instrumentation, voices, rhythms, and tempo to create a new sound (such as classical music arranged for a jazz orchestra). Arrangers have tremendous creative freedom.

When summer ended, Macy contemplated staying in New York to gain theater experience rather than returning to UF. But instead of quitting school entirely, she worked theater gigs in New York and attended classes in Gainesville or online. At UF everyone knew Macy as a 19-year-old student, but in New York she told people she was a 23-year-old professional so they wouldn't expect her to work for free. She says she "felt like Hannah Montana" straddling two communities and personas. But she has no regrets.

Upon graduation from UF, she was qualified to teach music theory at Pace University's New York City campus, and having established herself professionally, she had the income to afford New York rent and pursue her dream.

According to Macy, the biggest challenge in her industry is becoming known. Often still relying on cold emails, she "put a lot of energy into networking authentically and building relationships" with people she admired. She says, "The most life-changing relationships, opportunities, and mentorships that I have in my life have been from e-mailing someone and introducing myself."

Macy got more and more work as a music assistant, copyist, and music director. Happy with her performance, people rehired and recommended her. But the job she dreamed of—orchestrating—seemed out of reach.

For women, orchestration is the hardest Broadway music role to break into. Why? Because there's no "assistant orchestrator" stepping-stone position. The only way in is with a mentor. But theater orchestration is a predominantly male profession, and as in many industries, men have historically mentored other men.

Macy compiled a list of people who had orchestrated a Broadway show over the previous 20 years—190 in all. She found 90.5 percent were white men, 5.8 percent were BIPOC (Black, Indigenous, and People of Color) men, 3.7 percent were white women, and none were BIPOC women.

In a show Macy music supervised, *She Persisted, The Musical* (based on Chelsea Clinton's book), astronaut Sally Ride says, "You can't be what you can't see." Macy saw no one who looked like her among Broadway's orchestrators. Still, she persisted. In search of a mentor, Macy narrowed her list to "every living Tony-nominated orchestrator" and introduced herself to most of them. But no mentor emerged.

So, like piano, she taught herself orchestration and learned enough to get non-Broadway orchestration work.

In 2018, Macy orchestrated the play *Interstate*. In 2019, she music directed, arranged, and orchestrated "Passion Project: Love Songs from Women to Their Work," a song cycle by Angela Sclafani. She also orchestrated and arranged music for the musical comedy *It Came from Outer Space* for Chicago Shakespeare Theater.

Meanwhile, she was determined to get a music job—any job—with an actual Broadway show. This can be difficult. Musicals are developed over years of table reads, workshops, and out-of-town productions (see chapter 4 for more details), and when a show originating in the US hits Broadway, it usually arrives with an established music team.

But when she learned that *Tina: The Tina Turner Musical* was coming to Broadway from London's West End, Macy figured they wouldn't be bringing the whole London team over. She cold e-mailed the show's music supervisor, Nicholas Skilbeck, and her instinct proved correct. Nick hired her to music assist for *Tina* through the show's opening in November 2019, and she finished that job just before the COVID-19 pandemic hit the United States.

Then, on March 12, 2020, Broadway went dark.

Two months later, George Floyd was murdered by a police officer in Minneapolis, Minnesota, while three other officers failed to intervene, igniting months and months of mass protests attended by an estimated 21 million adult Americans—the largest mass protest in US history. Conversations about systemic racism and calls for justice and equity pervaded every corner of American life, including New York City theaters. Macy knew she couldn't fix it all, but there was one thing she could do.

All too often she'd seen highly qualified female musicians of color passed over for opportunities on Broadway. So, in the midst of the pandemic, 23-year-old Macy Schmidt became an agent of change. She founded and assembled The Broadway Sinfonietta, "an all female-identifying, majority women-of-color orchestral collective showcasing the excellence of BIPOC women musicians on Broadway and beyond."

The pandemic opened another door for Macy: with theaters shuttered, Broadway orchestrators actually had time to launch a New York branch of the American Society of Music Arrangers and Composers (ASMAC), which provides networking opportunities and supports the development of emerging orchestrators, arrangers, and composers in television, theater, and film scoring. ASMAC NYC started hosting webinars, and Macy jumped at the opportunity to learn from the best.

During one webinar, Macy asked Tony-nominated Broadway orchestrator Larry Blank, who orchestrated *Irving Berlin's White Christmas, Catch Me If You Can*, and more, for guidance on a chart she was working on. Larry offered to coach her through the score saying, "Let's get into the craft."

Craft! They were discussing craft! Macy finally had a mentor. Others followed, including Broadway orchestrator John Clancy, who orchestrated *Diana, Mean Girls*, and *Fun Home*.

She was learning at light speed—and just in time for the official launch of the Sinfonietta. "You're Gonna Hear from Me," a song written by André and Dory Previn, would be their first video recording.

Macy planned to orchestrate and produce the song, but how would she pay everyone else? She had an idea. She'd heard female Broadway producers talking to the press about their desire for change. So, she cold e-mailed them asking for help. Producers Jana Shea and Daryl Roth both responded immediately with donations, and Macy made her video.

On launch day, October 23, 2020, *CBS Sunday Morning* aired the Sinfonietta's "You're Gonna Hear from Me," featuring Zimbabwe-born American singer Solea Pfeiffer. The orchestra had liftoff. Watch the video. You'll hear a diverse cast of extraordinary musicians declaring to the world that they *will* be seen and heard.

Next, they made a Black History Month campaign video of George Gershwin's "Summertime" sponsored by MAC Cosmetics in partnership with Women of Color on Broadway.

Then came a Sinfonietta performance of Kesha Sebert's "Here Comes the Change," honoring the inauguration of Vice President Kamala Harris, arranged and orchestrated by Macy and performed by South Asian singer and Broadway star Shoba Narayan (who played Eliza Hamilton in *Hamilton*, Nessarose in *Wicked*, and Jasmine in *Aladdin*).

And with three beautifully produced videos as calling cards, here came the change for both the Sinfonietta and Macy. Bookings flowed in. Sometimes Macy is hired to orchestrate and suggests the Sinfonietta for the gig; sometimes the reverse happens.

Macy's Sinfonietta orchestrations caught the attention of producers of *Ratatouille: The TikTok Musical*, and when they invited her to orchestrate, she recommended the Sinfonietta.

"I had about 14 days to deliver 12 numbers orchestrated for a 20-piece orchestra," she recalls. "I would wake up every day, check my phone, turn my phone off for 12 to 15 hours, and then just not go to sleep till the song of the day was done." Finally, her part complete, Macy watched the show on New Year's Day, moved to tears by viewers' reactions.

Then came the *New York Times* review; theater critic Jesse Green said she'd orchestrated a "classic Disney Act I finale in the brassy manner of Alan Menken." A big compliment!

Macy made her debut in London's West End (Britain's Broadway) in 2021 as orchestrator for *Ride*—a musical about Annie Londonderry, the first woman to ride a bicycle around the world—and the Sinfonietta recorded the cast album. She was also included in the 2021 Women to Watch on Broadway list by the Broadway Women's Fund.

In 2022, Macy was selected by a panel of celebrity judges, including Miley Cyrus, for *Forbes'* 30 Under 30 Music list.

Best of all, in fall 2022, *Kimberly Akimbo*, a musical for which she provided additional orchestrations, will open on Broadway—making Macy a Broadway orchestrator at last.

Look out for Macy Schmidt. You'll find her name under orchestrator, arranger, music director, orchestra founder, conductor, and producer. All because . . . to Macy, "the relationship between the sound and the page is the coolest thing in the world."

Composers and Songwriters Macy Loves

- Kate Anderson and Elyssa Samsel, songwriting team for *Olaf's Frozen Adventure* and *Between the Lines*
- Kate Leonard, lyricist, and Daniel Mertzlufft, composer, for *Ratatouille: The TikTok Musical*
- Helen Park, composer of *KPOP* (the musical)
- Jeanine Tesori, composer of *Fun Home* (Tony Award winner) and *Kimberly Akimbo*

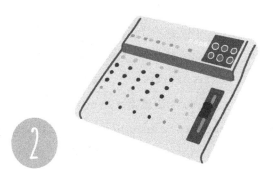

Lia Mice:
Innovating Inclusion

Artist, instrument designer, and all-around audio explorer Lia Mice travels the world performing in the most unusual venues: a military bunker in Munich, a clock tower in Manhattan, a boat in Lyon. And she's a repeat headliner at the electronic music festival in the Komyo-ji Temple in Tokyo.

The Australian-born, London-based artist makes music with technology old and new, self-designed and self-hacked, analog (samplers) and digital (multimedia software) and even eight-track tapes. Her shows are innovative, high-energy, and quirky.

When asked how long she's been obsessed with music, Lia answers simply, "Just always." Music is Lia's lifeline.

Lia is partially sighted—she has full vision in her right eye while her left is almost entirely blind. But doctors misdiagnosed this condition at birth as squint (when the eyes point in different directions, also known as strabismus), and she was forced to wear an eyepatch over her right eye to correct her left. During the years that Lia lived without sight, sound became central. She moved around her house using auditory cues. She relied on oral rather than written instructions at school. And she turned to music for solace in a world that didn't seem made for her.

Lia only escaped from her eye treatment—in fact, *mistreatment*—at age 10 by "cheating" on an eye exam. Glancing at the chart with her right eye, Lia quickly made up a song to help her memorize the letters. When it was time to test the left eye, she recited the song back. "So, yeah," Lia says, "music saved my life."

As a child, Lia lay in her bed at night listening to cassette tapes on a Sony Walkman, longing to live in the world where that music was getting made. "When I'm in control, I'll do whatever I want," she told herself. "When I'm old enough, I'll go live in that world."

And Lia made good on that promise.

She charged headlong into music because of her childhood experience. "I think my hearing developed in an amazing way because of being made to be blind for 10 years."

As soon as Lia could reach her mother's piano, she began playing (by ear). From there, Lia picked up guitar, performing in bands throughout high school.

She remembers the 1980s as a time with "such amazing electronic sounds happening." Lia played that music nonstop. "I'd just be listening to it over and over and over," she recalls. "I'd be like, 'oh, that's weird—the drums are changing in this'. . . . I was just analyzing the music production without knowing that's what I was doing."

As Lia got more and more into production, her music became more and more electronic. After college, she started playing full time, striking out as a solo artist. And then the touring began—Australia, the United States, Europe, Japan.

Lia estimates that she changed her setup 50 times while developing her live show. "I was constantly selling and buying secondhand gear to figure out the jigsaw of what my live set would be." Each technology upgrade allowed Lia to remix sound in increasingly novel ways.

Unlike players of instruments like the guitar or piano, electronic musicians rely on a variety of equipment. No two setups are the same. For Lia, it's all about creating "that" moment—the spontaneous musical excursion in an otherwise planned performance.

"Playing in bands, something that's really fun is when you all catch each other's eye, and you kind of like go off on a tangent," Lia explains. Performers who've practiced a piece many times together can surprise and delight audiences by changing it up—speeding it up or stretching it out or introducing chord variations. To do this kind of thing on stage alone, however, an electronic musician must engineer opportunities to improvise with herself.

Live Setup

Early in her stage career, Lia pulled beats off an iPod, layered in guitar with a looping pedal, and picked up vocals with a microphone. But she soon felt trapped by that technology—it was shaping her show. Lia couldn't even change the tempo or key of a song because the different sounds were simply looped (added) on top of each other.

As time went on and technology improved, Lia invested in samplers, which allow her to simultaneously create and modify many different channels of beats, bass, synths, percussion, etc. She can bring individual sounds in and out, pitch them up or down, or chop her voice until it stutters. "I'm able to completely live remix it every night," she says. "I can slow it right down and make it just a murky kind of ambient thing and then bust in the next song. It gives me so much flexibility."

Lia never plays the same show twice. "Why would I play the next show as it *was*?" Lia asks. "I'm going to play the next show as the *next version*."

Lia's inclination to innovate posed a challenge in 2011, however. That's the year she committed to recording her first solo album. But how could a single recording represent all that she could or would or wanted to be—all that she wanted to give a listener (like the headphone-clad kid she'd been) reaching for music in the dark? Also, Lia felt overly exposed by the idea of strangers listening to her music, knowing that she had made every creative decision—as though they could "tune in directly" to her brain. She recalls, "I think I was putting too much thought into what it was. I thought this one album was going to define who I am."

It was a question of artistic integrity and control. And when Lia set off for a performance in Tokyo that same year, concerns about the unfinished album followed her to the 30th Tasogare Festival, whispering in the dimly lit spaces of the Komyo-ji Temple.

Little did Lia know that's where she'd find the answer.

The Tasogare Festival is a unique event in which experimental music and traditional worship coexist. It started as a house party thrown by Takuya Endo and Shoukei Matsumoto, friends who'd organized music events together as college students. When Shoukei became a monk, he and Takuya invited a hundred or so guests to bring a favorite record to enjoy in the temple's main hall. The first played was Brian Eno's *Music for Airports*. In Lia's *Tasogare* documentary (available on her website), Takuya says, "I still remember how thrilling it was listening to Brian Eno in this religious space."

The festival's name has two meanings. *Tasogare* is an old and uncommon Japanese term that means "twilight." But when it's written in the Japanese kanji writing system, the characters translate to "who are you?" These ideas came together in ancient Japan—in a countryside that, before the advent of streetlights, grew very dark at the day's end. Back then, it was impossible to see whether a figure approaching was friend or foe. So, into the twilight, you'd call out, "Tasogare?"

This end-of-day inquiry is still practiced at the temple, and the response is fascinating. Lia explains, "If you're the person in the twilight and people can't see who you are, and they ask, 'Who are you?' you get to just decide—in that moment—this is who I am." You don't have to explain who you were five years ago or predict who you'll be tomorrow—your present self is enough.

As a child, Lia had longed for the power to define and redefine herself—to say who she was and what she could do. But she'd lived through a difficult and formative decade in which her voice wasn't heard. "In reality, being forced into looking out of my blind eye was very traumatic. And I couldn't get anyone to believe me that I was blind."

Many years later, as a professional artist, Lia stood on the Tasogare Festival stage encircled by candles and statuary. She sang softly into the mic. She strummed her guitar, looping the chord progression. And she listened to the music moving through the main hall, thinking, *This is the best my music has ever sounded.*

The Komyo-ji Temple is, in fact, famed for its acoustics. It was designed for sound—for the chant-based meditation practiced in Shin Buddhism. These acoustic properties allow monks to connect with the musicality of their chanting, which in turn deepens the meaning. Lia experienced this in the festival's finale—a group chant. It was as if time slowed down for her to take it all in.

She knelt on the floor before an open chant book.

She read the words aloud and in unison with others.

She listened to the slow decay of sound across the meditation space.

This is beautiful, she thought, *but it's not* designed *to be beautiful.*

Although people weren't trying to chant in tune, all the mismatched vocal tones came together in that moment. Anyone listening carefully could hear it: a sacred event was unfolding. And it unlocked something inside Lia.

She realized that whether something sounded special or not depended on how closely you listened. And that insight is what Lia needed to finish her album: "I can't make this album for everybody," she realized. "I just have to be okay with how *I* think it sounds."

After the festival, Lia rushed home to her studio. "I started making my album really slow, like 80 BPM [beats per minute], to give space for things to decay in-between the beats. And playing at that edgy tempo really affected my creative process at that time." Since the release of that album, *Happy New Year*, Lia has recorded another three—*I Love You* (2014), *The Sampler as a Time Machine* (2018), and *Sweat Like Caramel* (2022).

Music reviewers call Lia a "pioneer of experimental pop." They draw on a wide variety of genres to describe her work—electro, tech noir, and industrial. And beyond labels are lovely snapshots like this, offered by *Tiny Mix Tapes*: "Lia Mice makes lush pop music, delicate and colorful like cherry petals in the wind—but she's a strong believer in the power of noise and the beauty of the destroyed tape."

Lia is a recipient of numerous residencies, including the Innovative Instrument Design—Du Xian Qin International Workshop at the China Conservatory of Music, Estalagem da Ponta do Sol Residency for Contemporary Music and Electronics on Madeira Island, and Automation and Me at the Leeds International Festival of Ideas.

In 2015, she founded London's Electrolights AV—an experimental platform highlighting audio-visual artists and performers, which she continues to curate. This art collective has featured talent including La Leif, A'Bear, digitalselves, Natalie Sharp/Lone Taxidermist, Zachary Aghaizu, and Loraine James.

In 2021, Lia received a prestigious Oram Award. The awards provide a platform for innovation in sound, music, and related technologies to elevate the work and voices of women, girls, and gender minority music creators in electronic music.

Though Lia has clearly made it to the world of music that called to her as a child, she doesn't stop there. Alongside her career as an artist, Lia makes instruments.

Her instrument design training began organically. Forever curious about what makes things work, Lia took apart cassette players, rewired speakers, and tinkered with guitar pedals.

She followed instrument designers online, including artist and engineer Andy Cavatorta, who collaborated with Björk on the robotic musical instrument dubbed the "Gravity Harp" for her Biophilia Tour in 2010. Lia felt awe at the sight—and sound— of that instrument, with its four pendulums hanging 25 feet in the air and playing notes as they slowly swung back and forth.

For the longest time, the engineering expertise to build something like that felt out of reach to Lia—like something you just had to be born with. But as time went by, she discovered the truth: "You figure it out as you do it."

Through fixing her own equipment and producing her own music, competence gave rise to confidence. In 2015, Lia moved to London to do a Masters of Music in Creative Practice at Goldsmiths, University of London. During a class called Interactive and Generative Music, she built Soul Delay, an interactive musical world map. The project represented a milestone—evidence that she had the chops for instrument design. Soon after, Lia began doctoral work in the Media and Arts Technology program at Queen Mary University of London, where she joined the Augmented Instruments Lab.

Entering a STEM field at this level put Lia on a steep learning curve. And she is one of few women in her field. A 2017 study from the United Kingdom showed that only 16 percent of people working in STEM are female. In music tech that number falls to 5 percent. But Lia's example is reason for optimism, and she encourages girls to follow in her footsteps: "This world is so ready to welcome more women."

For Lia, the most exciting thing about new electronic technologies like microprocessors and sensors is that they enable design of instruments that can be customized and personalized. "There is no such thing as an instrument that all people can perform," Lia says, "and there is no such thing as an average musician." So, she employs a collaborative design process—a process that listens to the voices of individual musicians, particularly players with disabilities—and learns from them to create better musical instruments:

> Nobody knows their own body better than themselves. Yet too often instruments, or for that matter all types of things, are designed "for" rather than "by" disabled people. This disregards the knowledge that disabled people have about our own bodies and what works best for us and is why the disabled community is calling for "nothing about us without us."

In 2018, Lia began a collaboration with the One-Handed Musical Instrument (OHMI) Trust, whose goal is to redesign traditional instruments so they can be played with only one hand. OHMI identified the need for a one-handed violin from their community members who were frustrated with school music lessons that taught all students to play the same instrument (often the violin) without consideration for students who have a disability that affects an upper limb.

Lia's one-handed violin allows players to produce a full range of sound using only their bowing arm. The key design question was how to shift the violin's pitch without relying on the second hand to select notes on the fingerboard. A foot pedal might seem an obvious option, but a lot of people who don't have control of both arms also lack the foot dexterity required for this task. Instead, Lia decided to use the voice.

While bowing the one-handed violin, the musician quietly sings or hums the desired note. Their voice is picked up by a neck microphone and passed onto a microcomputer that recognizes the sung tones and pitch-shifts the instrument's sound to match. It's possible to do this without perceivable delays so it appears as if the music is a direct result of contact between the violin strings and bow hairs.

Lia is quick to point out that her one-handed violin isn't a complete design—rather, it's a proof of concept. It opens discussions about how to create even more accessible instruments through collaborative design.

Instrument Innovation

A key supporter of Lia's instrument design work at the University of London is her PhD supervisor, Professor Andrew McPherson. An electrical engineer and classically trained musician, Andrew's research centers around creating new expressive tools for musicians, including electronically augmented acoustic instruments.

Laurel S. Pardue, creator of the award-winning violin learning device Svampolin, has also been an academic ally. She shared design expertise and the computer code underlying Lia's one-handed violin.

Rachel Wolffsohn, general manager at the OHMI Trust, advised Lia about what makes a well-designed, one-handed instrument—knowledge that can only be gained from lived experience of upper limb disability.

Visit Lia's website to explore her other instruments, including ChandeLIA, Prism Bell, and Chaos Bells, which won the "Highly Commended" Award in Best Innovation of a Sound Tool or Technique at the 2021 Sound of the Year Awards.

A theme running through all of Lia's work as an artist, instrument designer, and academic is inclusion. She's a big believer in the power of music to bring people together.

The event in the Komyo-ji Temple is a great example. "I never would think, 'Oh, I can just go to a temple and make friends with monks,'" Lia says. "But they love music, I love music, so, of course, we can be friends."

Lia finds this attitude reflected around the globe: "I've been fortunate to perform in fifteen countries so far, and something I've noticed is if you like music, there are people all around the world who are ready to be your friend. . . . You're never alone."

Katarina Benzova: Shooting Stars

For rock photographer and documentarian Katarina "Kat" Benzova, "there are moments that happen on stage, moments of sheer bliss. . . . Music is flowing through the musicians and connects with the audience."

In breathtaking black-and-white photography, Kat has captured spiritual high points for bands such as Guns N' Roses, AC/DC, Aerosmith, the Rolling Stones, KISS, and ZZ Top, to name just a few.

In this chapter, you'll read the story of the artist *behind* the lens—Kat's journey to the stars.

Her success happened overnight, literally. Before the nine o'clock concert on September 18, 2010, at the 16,000-seater Wiener Stadthalle arena in Vienna, Austria, Kat had never sold a photo, never purchased professional photography equipment, and never shot from the wings of a stadium stage. But there she was, stage left, using a VIP pass provided by a friend to photograph Guns N' Roses (GNR) with her little point-and-shoot camera.

"Shooting that one concert," Kat says, "I discovered a talent that I didn't know I had." Others saw her talent too—in fact, none other than GNR front man Axl Rose.

The stadiums hosting tens of thousands of screaming rock fans where Kat now practices her art contrast sharply with the tranquil town of her childhood. But there, in the Liptov region of Slovakia, is where she developed an eye for beauty that would one day take her around the world.

Kat explored the mountains of her beloved homeland before she could even walk or talk—from a snug spot in her grandmother's backpack. Later, a favorite outing was trekking through the woods in search of herbs and berries. And mushrooming became a tradition for three generations of Benzova women. Kat recounts, "The whole family connects in silence with nature and each other, having the same goal of finding the biggest porcini. It's really meditative." By spending her childhood in nature, Kat learned to sense and observe her surroundings.

Photography was still years away for Kat, and rock music from the wider world was only starting to trickle into what was then postcommunist Slovakia. But Kat heard classical music played at the ice-skating rink. And her dance lessons—ballet, contemporary jazz, and Slovakian folk—were accompanied by live piano and accordion music. Kat especially loved her dance school with its little bench in the courtyard. She'd arrive early just to sit and listen. "You could hear a beautiful chaos of sounds from all the classrooms."

"I think my dreams were pretty normal for a little girl: a princess, vet, ballerina, or a professional figure skater as my mom," Kat says. But she quickly outgrew ice-skating—literally—because her mom couldn't afford to keep replacing skates.

At the age of 13, a family friend suggested a new possibility: modeling. Athletic Kat had no interest in fashion, but she reluctantly agreed to attend a local contest held by Elite Model Management. To Kat's surprise, she left that competition with an offer from the biggest modeling agency in the world—and one that operated in the world's biggest cities, including Paris, Milan, and Tokyo.

Until then, Kat had only ever left Slovakia to visit neighboring Poland and the Croatian coast. But she was curious about the bustling urban centers of Europe, Asia, and the Americas. "I've always been an adventurous and independent type," she explains. "I grew up as an only child without a father. So, I was used to being alone, easily adaptable, with zero issues meeting new people or asking for directions when I was lost."

The decision to sign the modeling contract was easy for Kat, but not so for her mother, Iveta. "I will be forever thankful that she had let me go," Kat says.

The permission to travel came with a condition, however: Kat had to continue her education. To keep that promise in the days before distance learning, she qualified for an independent study program from a local academy. Only Kat and one other girl from school—an Olympic skier—were granted this plan.

Kat packed photocopies of classmates' handwritten notes to prep for test-taking between trips. But her on-the-road education entailed so much more.

When kids travel these days, they have many ways to stay connected—map apps and search engines for navigation, voice and text and video for communication. By contrast, Kat called her mom once a week from a payphone on the street and got to modeling appointments using paper maps and metro tickets. "During fashion weeks, you have ten to fifteen castings a day to get to on your own in a city you don't know," she explains. "You learn fast on your own mistakes. You learn time management and discover the most magical places all around the world when you get lost."

Kat also discovered languages. "When I lived in Tokyo, I had to learn Japanese," she recalls. "My English was so bad, and obviously nobody spoke Slovakian."

Despite these challenges—or maybe because of them—Kat feels she attended "the best school of life."

This schooling exposed Kat to music. "I never saw MTV when I was growing up and basically I just started to learn about music from radio and when I started to travel the world at 14."

And of course, this education involved photography.

Picture-taking started simply: Kat brought a camera and two rolls of film on each trip as a way to share her adventures with her family. In those days, the cost of film processing required Kat to make a limited number of exposures last. And that restriction turned out to be a gift. That's how she developed her instinct to wait—for just the right moment—before clicking.

Kat's photography skills also got a boost from her hours of modeling in front of the camera. "When you're constantly surrounded by creative and inspiring people, it helps you to see the world in a different way."

But as Kat's interest in taking pictures grew, the appeal of posing for them wore off. "You are circled by outside beauty and that becomes boring after a while, so you start to dig deeper and search for more."

Kat wasn't afraid of change. Her mother taught her that. At the age of 45, Iveta went back to school to earn a master's degree in social work. "She got the best she could be in something, and then it wasn't enough."

Wondering what her own next "best" would be, Kat took stock of her interests—sports, music, and photography. Having completed her education during a decade on the road, Kat started looking for work in her favorite cities.

She DJed in Tokyo and Singapore nightclubs. Later, a friend opened a swimming instruction school in Los Angeles, so Kat flew out, got certified, and taught lessons by day while DJing at night.

Kat was combining things she loved but wasn't loving her life. Plus, it was hard to make a living in L.A. So, in 2010, she returned home—to Slovakia and her roots. "I took a step back from everything and concentrated on NOW, not the next steps into the future," she explains.

And that's when it happened: An old friend called to invite Kat to the Guns N' Roses concert in Vienna. Carrying a little point-and-shoot camera, she set out to meet him. Kat was excited to hear the music, but the idea of *seeing* the musicians—through the lens of her camera—thrilled her:

> There was never an emotional connection when I was on the other side of the lens. I was a hanger for clothes as a model. But that's not the reason why I started to seek deeper connection. I didn't even know I was seeking it until I started to shoot my first shows. I found out I can connect to the wavelength of the performing artist and their emotions. Some sort of empathy, I guess. Annie Leibovitz once said that she's not afraid to fall in love with the people she photographs. It's kind of like that. . . . I'm really sensitive and I observe. I see the beauty in facial expressions and movement, and I connect to it.

Moved by the Vienna concert images that Kat posted on social media, the band connected with her online. Next, the

GNR management invited Kat to a show in Prague. That's where she met Axl Rose. After the concert, they chatted about art and photography. Kat remembers it something like this:

Kat: "I took some photos at the last show. And the guys from the band liked them. They started to follow me on Facebook."

Axl: "We're actually looking for a photographer right now."

Kat (joking): "So, hire me as your photographer."

Axl: "You know what? That's actually not a bad idea."

Did we just make a deal? Kat wondered. Probably not, she decided on the way home. But a few days later, GNR's management called to invite her to Spain for two tryout shows.

Kat: "You've got to be kidding me? This is not happening!"

But it was. And she went. And they hired her.

Was this destiny or just fortuitous timing? For Kat, there's no difference. "I believe everything happens for a reason. You get opportunities presented to you throughout your life and then it's just up to you if you have the courage to take it and leap into the unknown. And once you take it, you have to work hard to keep it."

Kat suddenly found herself among professional photographers who'd studied for many years and steered careers through many smaller band gigs. By contrast, Kat borrowed a DSLR (digital single-lens reflex) camera to bring on her first tour and learned how to use it during a weekend of YouTube tutorials. "I had an eye for it, just needed to learn how to capture it technically," Kat explains. She developed her unique style by trial and error, undaunted by the idea of learning while doing.

Kat's on-the-job ed also included a crash course in stage production. Light, shadows, and movement—these things she understood from modeling. But rock concerts with dancing and running, confetti and pyrotechnics, were a whole new level. Concert photographers must be stealthy on stage. A sure way to lose a gig—or worse, to cause an accident—is to mess with the choreography of a performance.

But documenting a tour isn't just about shooting a show. Fans want to see rehearsals, travel, and after-parties as well. In these moments, stealth and sensitivity are required too. Kat has to know the musicians—their personalities, habits, and moods. If you distract performers in their backstage sanctuary, that can also affect a show.

Tour Photographer

Ask Kat to describe a day in the life of a tour photographer and she'll tell you to pick your adventure. Is it a travel or performance day? Are you going by tour bus, commercial flight, or private jet? Is the venue a club, stadium, or festival grounds?

On the morning of a stadium concert, for example, Kat has breakfast and visits the gym because it's important to stay healthy on the road. Then she goes back to her hotel room and edits images from the day before.

As showtime approaches, Kat chooses an outfit from a small suitcase of jeans, tops, sneakers, boots, rain jackets, and comfy hoodies. A tour photographer must be ready for all kinds of weather with a varied wardrobe of outfits—all black, of course.

Before the concert, Kat shoots the soundcheck. And she usually stays at the stadium to continue editing rather than rest up at the hotel.

Soon, fans arrive and it's time to record interviews for social media.

At last, the show starts, and with GNR, that's a three-hour photo shoot.

Afterward, as musicians celebrate or sleep on the jet, what's the tour photographer doing? Editing, of course!

Kat was surprised to discover how much her early years of fashion travel prepared her for life as a rock photographer. "Stage, audience, traveling, staying at the same hotel, weeks or months with the same people," she recounts. "Everything was the same but different. Even the amount of partying is probably the same." But there are far fewer women in rock photography.

It's still a male-dominated industry. It took time for Kat to be accepted by the "wolf pack," and she has to show her "horns" sometimes to gain respect. When someone makes an ignorant comment, another thing Kat shows is her work.

"I know my worth," she says. "I know how much hard work it took to get where I am and to stay there."

You, too, can see her work in periodicals like *Rolling Stone*, *Vogue*, and the *New York Times*, as well as the Rock Photography Museum online and her own gorgeous website.

One of the first things you'll notice is Kat's use of black-and-white to capture the rock concert atmosphere. That choice allows her to amplify emotion and minimize visual distractions (like fire, lights, and confetti). Her work show-cases those moments when artists are "like lightning rods, receiving and transmitting the energy of the universe for all to hear."

When a fan looks at one of Kat's photographs and exclaims, "Oh, I feel I'm right there," she rejoices. Mission accomplished. More than a lovely photo, she wants people to experience the beauty of the music, to sense a connection with the musicians.

Kat's ability to conduct electricity from the stage is cele-brated by artists as well as fans.

Steven Tyler of Aerosmith says, "I've seen a million photos of me screaming, but this one is different. It's like she saw right into my soul."

John Tempesta of the Cult describes Kat as "one of the best rock photographers of our generation."

And Hard Rock Hotel displayed Kat's KISS photos next to stills by legendary photographers Bob Gruen, Lynn Goldsmith, and Neal Preston. "That was the biggest honor I could have received," Kat recalls. To take a new and noteworthy photo of KISS in the same make-up and costumes they've worn for 40 years is not easy.

When Kat looks back on the decade since that first concert in Vienna, she sums up her experience like this: "I've been on the road for the past 10 years almost nonstop. I am a woman in a male-dominated industry, my career was never easy. But I love challenges and proving gender equality. . . . My mission in life is to give back. I got an opportunity and certain amount of talent and want to do what I can to use it to make this world a better place."

What does outreach look like for a busy tour photographer?

When she's on the road, Kat might use a rare hour off to help a local animal shelter. "Did you know that animals from animal shelters have higher chances to get adopted if they have better photos online? Me neither," Kat says. "So, I did that."

Kat also donates prints and creative time to organizations such as Legacy of Hope (Nelson Mandela's foundation), Janie's Fund, the Heroes Project, the Wolf Conservation Center, and CREW Nation.

In 2017, Kat established her own foundation, Mission11, which creates campaigns with video, photography, and even celebrity support for organizations fighting for the planet. For example, to help Animals Asia save moon bears from bile farms, Mission11 flipped the animal cruelty narrative. Instead of heartbreaking photos, Kat snapped funny ones. The campaign, entitled "Let a Bear Sh!t in the Woods," features shots of rock stars in furry costumes and fierce poses. Check it out on the Mission11 website.

Kat's philanthropy is one example of the many ways that professional photographers can make the world a better place while doing what they love.

For aspiring music photographers, her advice is this: shoot, shoot, shoot, and make connections. "Don't be afraid that you're going to be turned down, because you will. That's a part of this job. You will be turned down so many times, but that one time is going to work. And you don't know where it's going to take you."

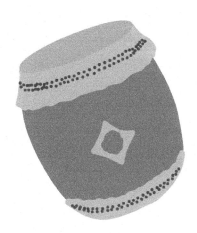

Part II
Power to Perform

Janet Dacal: Hitting Broadway Heights

Janet Dacal walked into The Drama Book Shop on West 39th Street for her very first audition in New York City. Pacing nervously outside the shop's basement theater, she heard the distinct sound of a piano. When her turn came, she entered the tiny theater and sang the song she'd prepared.

The guy at the piano must have liked what he heard, because he invited Janet to stay. Then he played an unfamiliar song, pounding out the chords and singing the vocals.

Could Janet sing that?

Of course she could! It had a Latin rhythm—perfect for a Cuban American singer like her.

Janet sang.

The pianist played another tune.

Again Janet sang.

Back and forth they went.

By the end of the session, Janet had the job.

It was 2002. The piano player was Lin-Manuel Miranda. And the audition was for a very early table read of his musical *In the Heights*—a show that would change both their lives.

How did a first-generation Latina from L.A. find her way to the New York stage? It started with the word "yes."

Music was always playing in the Dacal home, and from the time she could stand, Janet danced and sang along. To channel that energy, her parents asked if she'd like dance lessons at a neighborhood studio. Janet said yes—to tap, ballet, and later, jazz.

Janet's immigrant parents, Mercedes and Lazaro Armando Dacal, were adamant that she pursue her passions because— unlike in Cuba—in the United States, she could. She says, "Having that in my ear all the time gave me permission to do things, knowing they were supportive of whatever I chose."

In fourth grade, Janet auditioned to sing in the chorus for the school play, *Snow White*. But Mr. Pedraja, the drama teacher, wanted her to try a speaking role.

He handed her the script, and Janet read the lines. Then she stopped, unsure of herself.

The stage direction in the script read, *She sobs uncontrollably.* Sobs? What were sobs?

"You have to pretend to cry," Mr. Pedraja explained.

Janet fell to her knees and wailed.

She was cast as Snow White.

Acting felt natural to Janet, like, "Oh, this is my glass slipper . . . this fits well." Mr. Pedraja recognized her talent. Knowing her family had very little means, he encouraged her to audition for a public performing-arts middle school, and she got in.

Next, Janet attended the Academy of Music & Performing Arts at Hamilton High School in L.A. Every morning Janet rode the 5:30 AM school bus from South Gate on L.A.'s east side to Hamilton on the west. She would arrive at school, take classes all day, attend an afterschool dance program, attend evening practice at a private dance studio, get home around eleven o'clock at night, fall into bed, catch the 5:30 AM bus the next day, and do it all over again. She loved it!

At Hamilton, Janet found a diverse, like-minded community. "What bonded us was how much we loved art and dancing and music," she recalls.

Janet completed tenth grade at Hamilton. Then her parents divorced, and Janet, her mother, and two brothers moved to Miami, Florida. Although it was hard to leave her friends in L.A., she adjusted easily. They lived in a neighborhood where everyone was Cuban like her, where people spoke Spanish the way she did, and where the taste of cortaditos (coffees), pastelitos (pastries), and croquetas (meat-filled croquettes) lit up her taste buds and fed her soul.

Janet attended the local high school and participated in its theater program. An alumnus of the high school, Henry Gainza, directed one of Janet's first high school shows. Later, he would play an important role in launching her career.

After graduating from high school, Janet studied broadcast journalism at Florida International University in Miami. She also worked as a receptionist at Crescent Moon Studios, a recording studio owned by Emilio and Gloria Estefan, the first mega-successful Latin crossover artists in the United States (see sidebar on page 170). Rising Latin stars of the 1990s, including Marc Anthony, Jennifer Lopez, Ricky Martin, and Shakira, were in the studio every day. It was an exciting time in music. Of course, Janet too wanted to be discovered, but she knew it was best to be discreet and respectful.

The building had a spiral staircase "with amazing reverb" where she often sang when she took the stairs. One day a studio songwriter heard Janet singing and invited her to step into a recording booth. *This is it!* she thought.

"This" turned out to be session singing, recording background vocals for artists, and making demos for the Crescent Moon songwriters. Singing at the studio, Janet developed a sense of her voice and what it could do.

"You're in a booth, isolated, by yourself with headphones," she says. "All you hear is your own voice. You're learning to manipulate sound and air and vulnerability. You're trying to get a story across only using your voice, trying to be intimate, or trying to really express a feeling by opening your instrument and making it very loud and powerful."

Meanwhile, Henry Gainza, whom Janet calls "one of my angels," landed an Off-Broadway show in New York titled *4 Guys Named José . . . and Una Mujer Named Maria.* One day, he phoned Janet with news: "They're bringing the show from New York to Miami. Are you interested in auditioning?"

A musical review of Latin songs, *4 Guys* includes "Mi Tierra," a song that her boss, Gloria Estefan, made famous. Janet auditioned and was cast as Maria.

"The bug bit hard when I stepped into that role because it was just the alignment of all of the things that I love, not just singing but dancing, and I'm telling a story and acting," Janet recalls.

Now she was working at the studio, going to school, and holding down her first professional acting job.

Gloria and Emilio saw the show. The following day, Gloria pulled Janet aside and told her, "You need to be doing *that*. That's where you belong."

"That" was musical theater.

Janet knew Gloria was right, so she asked Henry Gainza about getting auditions in New York. Always her angel, Henry set up Janet's fateful first audition—the one at The Drama Book Shop with his friend Lin-Manuel Miranda. At that time, 2002, Lin-Manuel was an unknown kid, fresh out of Wesleyan University, trying to mount his first show, *In the Heights*. Its blend of Latin music and dance, hip-hop, rap, and musical theater was the perfect vehicle for celebrating everything Janet loved. She not only did that first table read but also would continue to work with Lin-Manuel and the cast to develop the show over the coming months and years.

What Is a Table Read?

A table read takes place when the cast of a show gets together and reads through the script. For a musical, they also sing the songs, accompanied by the music director on piano. The creative team—scriptwriter, songwriter, director, producer, casting director, etc.—listens for strengths and weaknesses in the story, dialogue, songs, and pacing. Table reads are also a way to inspire investors.

Meanwhile, still in college and working at the studio, Janet flew to New York for other auditions. One-way flights were cheap. She'd fly in, audition, wait a few days for a "callback" (a request to audition a second time), then buy a return ticket.

She says, "I was so green. I didn't know what I was doing. I auditioned for all of these shows that were way out of my league. And it was an incredible experience."

During that period, Janet also went on a South American tour as a background singer for Latin salsa artist Luis Enrique, whose band played Latin jazz. Performing jazz, which entails a lot of improvisation, is very different from musical theater, "where everything is fine-tuned to perfection . . . and rehearsed down to a breath," says Janet. On tour, she never knew what would come next. That tour was a master class in musical improvisation.

After the tour, Janet continued flying to New York for auditions. Finally, after two years of commuting, she moved to Manhattan for what she assumed would be a brief stint. She didn't expect much to come of the experiment, but her then-husband was touring with a Latin pop star, and she figured she'd have some fun auditioning while he was on the road.

In 2005, Janet booked a job in the ensemble of the Broadway show *Good Vibrations*, which featured Beach Boys music. It only ran for 94 performances, but she'd made her Broadway debut.

Meanwhile, Janet says *In the Heights* was slowly "being developed and being developed and being developed." The cast would do a reading or present a workshop (perform the play in a rehearsal room with staging, choreography, minimal costumes, sets, and props, and even a band), then not see each other for months. Sometimes they went away for the summer to work on the show.

To learn more about how *In the Heights was developed*, read Lin-Manuel's book, *In the Heights: Finding Home* or watch the PBS *Great Performances* episode "In the Heights: Chasing Broadway Dreams."

Finally, after years of development, *In the Heights* premiered at the 2005 National Music Theater Conference with Janet originating the role of Carla—a "Chilean-Cuban-Dominican-Puerto Rican beautician" who has a beguiling innocence about her.

In 2007, *In the Heights* opened Off-Broadway. The cast, including Janet, won a Drama Desk Award for Outstanding Ensemble Performance, proving the show worthy of a Broadway stage.

The few months between the Off-Broadway closing and Broadway opening of *In the Heights* were "a time of deep, deep growth" for Janet. She graduated from college, got divorced, traveled alone in Europe, and spent time reflecting on her life. Then she was back onstage.

In the Heights won four 2008 Tony Awards including Best Musical. It was one of three finalists for the 2009 Pulitzer Prize for Drama. And the Broadway cast album, on which Janet sings, won a Grammy Award.

Janet eventually left *In the Heights* to originate the starring role, Alice, in the musical *Wonderland*. Putting her stamp on a new role is her favorite part of being an actor. She says, "There are things innately about you that you don't even realize are now part of that character forever."

Wonderland opened on Broadway in 2011. Janet got good reviews (listen to the Broadway cast album and you'll hear why), but the show itself had issues. It was not a hit and closed after two months.

"It was very easy to be discouraged about the trajectory the show was on," says Janet, "but I quickly came to realize that, as the show's lead, my energy affects everybody around me. People are looking at me for how to be." Inspired by her *In the Heights* colleagues Priscilla Lopez and Olga Merediz, Janet grew enormously as a leader.

Working with Her Heroes

Veteran actors Priscilla Lopez and Olga Merediz were in the cast of *In the Heights* for its entire Broadway run. Priscilla, a Tony Award winner, is best known for originating the role of Diana Morales in *A Chorus Line*. Olga, who has decades of stage and screen credits, received a Tony nomination for playing Abuela Claudia in *In the Heights*, a role she reprised in the movie version.

"That's the thing about this career, if you stick around long enough, you get to work with your heroes," says Janet. "So many of us were young and new on the scene, so to have Priscilla and Olga as our examples of how to be was priceless. Their composure, their energy in a room, how they carry themselves, how they revere the art form. They've been such anchors, not just for the theater, but for Latin women."

After *Wonderland*, Janet returned to the Broadway cast of *In the Heights* as Nina, a principal character, who is the first in her immigrant family to attend college, a situation Janet experienced herself as a first-generation college graduate.

After playing Nina, Janet moved back to Los Angeles to spend time with her dad. Although she went on auditions there, she says, "I just couldn't find my footing artistically." However, she did meet a kindred spirit in L.A., music arranger Carlos José Alvarez, who shared her vision for making an album of standards sung to Cuban-flavored arrangements.

After five years in L.A., Janet felt the tug of New York and moved back. Within three months, she'd booked *Prince of*

Broadway, a musical revue showcasing the producing career of Broadway legend Harold (Hal) Prince, who, at 91, directed the show. It was his last.

In *Prince of Broadway*, Janet played four completely different lead characters: Eva Perón from *Evita*, Aurora from *Kiss of the Spider Woman*, Young Sally from *Follies*, and Sydney from *It's a Bird . . . It's a Plane . . . It's Superman*. She also played small parts in other scenes. In all, she had 16 costume changes.

She recalls Hal's direction during a rehearsal for the *Evita* segment: "In the middle of me singing 'Argentina,' Hal says, in his very Hal way, 'She's a queen!' So simple, but it was everything I needed to hear."

A life in musical theater has its ups and downs. Janet books a lot of short runs: three months performing out of town, then home. It's a constant cycle of auditions, performances, then back to no work. In the process, Janet has learned some needed lessons about managing money.

She has been fortunate, rarely needing a nontheatrical job. But in the early years, she worked as a gym receptionist and as a coat checker, and for exactly one afternoon, she waited tables ("it didn't go well").

For years, Janet based her self-worth on her ability to earn a living through performing only. That changed when she asked herself, "How are you continuing your conversation about being an artist and developing your skill while you're waiting for the next big thing?"

Janet found her answer in Elizabeth Gilbert's book, *Big Magic: Creative Living Beyond Fear*, which gave her permission to explore new professional avenues. She began to teach and discovered that teaching makes her a better artist and working on her art makes her a better teacher.

In 2019, Janet landed her "dream" role: Dina, in the Broadway touring company of *The Band's Visit*, one of the most Tony Award–winning musicals ever. The show's website says, "[It] rejoices in the way music makes us laugh, makes us cry, and ultimately, brings us together."

Before starting the tour, Janet finally recorded that album of popular songs with Cuban arrangements so she could promote it on the road. Carlos José Alvarez wrote the arrangements in L.A., Janet recorded the vocals in New York, her niece recorded vocals in Australia, the musicians recorded in L.A. and Miami, and the album was mixed in Mexico. Still, they finished it in a month and a half. Titled *My Standards*, Janet says it's "an homage and just a great big thank you to my parents."

The album complete, Janet began touring with *The Band's Visit* in January 2020. But in March, theaters across the United States closed due to COVID-19. During the hiatus, Janet taught musical theater classes online, which was "a real lifeline." She began to mentor young Latinx performers. And she joined a cast of more than 100 Latinx artists for a virtual concert titled *¡Viva Broadway! Hear Our Voices* that raised over $189,000 for Latinx charities.

During the shutdown, the film version of *In the Heights* was released in movie theaters. Although she did not act in the film, Janet's voice can be heard on the soundtrack. And when the Broadway cast gathered for a screening, Janet was there:

> We love each other so much. It was a primarily Latinx cast, telling a Latinx story with this incredible music, depicting us as we are—hardworking contributors to society—and the heart and the joy that we experience every day. How lucky am I that that is the family that came into my life not only to catch me during the hardest times but to really celebrate who we are as a people and what we bring to the world!

From fall 2021 through 2022, Janet was back on tour, starring in *The Band's Visit*. You can watch her performing the show's signature song, "Omar Sharif," on YouTube.

What happens when the tour ends? Who knows? But whatever future roles await Janet, she can trace them all back to saying yes.

Yes to a life in musical theater.

Yes to an audition in the basement of a tiny book shop.

And yes a million times over to telling stories through song.

5

Valérie Sainte-Agathe:
Stronger Together

When Valérie Sainte-Agathe, conductor of the world-renowned San Francisco Girls Chorus, led her singers to the stage at the Yerba Buena Center for the Ars theater on February 29, 2020, everyone was feeling strength in numbers. "Choral music is about gathering and personalities," Valérie explains. "When we are together, we're strong."

That night, 40 singers from the chorus and 30 dancers from the Berkeley Ballet Theater joined forces to celebrate the 100th anniversary of American women's right to vote. The concert, Rightfully Ours, showcased the chorus's vocal power with pieces ranging from "Panda Chant," a song from Meredith Monk's science fiction opera, to "I Shouldn't Be Up Here," Angélica Negrón's response to the climate crisis, to "Herring Run," Carla Kihlstedt's musical exploration of ancestral knowledge and individual will.

In addition to beautiful music, what was on display in Rightfully Ours was Valérie's core artistic belief—namely, that children have something important to say: "It's about trusting them and training them and giving them the confidence to know that they can go out there and change everything."

Since joining the chorus in 2013, Valérie has been calling for an ever-widening range of music for treble voices (singers 4–18 years old). But in early 2020, she wasn't ready for the work of conducting a chorus through the silence of social distancing.

Rightfully Ours was her last in-person event of the year. "It was a beautiful project," Valérie remembers. "We were just in that joy of the collaboration, and then the lockdown. And it was scary."

The pandemic hit the music industry hard. Choral singing—an activity that requires intense breathing combined with vocal projection, often in crowded indoor spaces—was considered one of the highest-risk activities for the spread of COVID-19. Following tragic reports of rehearsals that turned into super-spreader events, choirs were among the first groups to pause, making the pandemic even more unnervingly quiet for the one in six Americans who regularly sang with others.

But Valérie's message in March 2020 was loud and clear: "The San Francisco Girls Chorus is almost 40 years old. It won't stop with me being director. So, we've got to figure it out."

If you ask Valérie where she gets that unrelenting drive to make music, she'll point to the tiny Caribbean island of Martinique, her childhood home. "In Martinique, the culture is music," she explains. There are events like Carnival, where everybody dresses up and celebrates in the streets. "It's a very uplifted community. The people from the islands have a sense of no matter what happens, everything's gonna be fine."

This attitude derives, in part, from the resilience of island people who live with an ongoing threat of natural disaster. "When I was younger, every summer you had a hurricane, and that would destroy everything," Valérie recalls. "And what do you do? You just rebuild, and that's it. You just don't stop. I have always been surrounded by this spirit—a very positive energy. And in the music, it was the same."

Musical Martinique

Martinique's music is a blend of French, West Indian, and African influences.

Valérie's neighbor, Ralph Thamar, was the longtime lead singer of the Malavoi ensemble, which combined traditional music from Martinique with classical music. "This is where my idea of mixing the different styles and cultures is coming from," Valérie remembers.

Another influence was Dédé Saint Prix, a popular percussionist who performs traditional chouval bwa, a kind of folk music and dance that originated among enslaved peoples working on island plantations.

Valérie was also a fan of Jacob Desvarieux, cofounder of the group Kassav, whose wildly popular song "Zouk-la-sé Sel Médikaman Nou Ni" started the zouk dance craze across the islands and into Latin America.

You can find videos of all three musicians on YouTube.

Though Valérie's parents weren't musicians, her mother, Armancy, loved piano and enrolled her only daughter in lessons. And her father, Christian, ensured that she practiced her scales and repertoire. "My journey is the result of real family effort!" she says.

While studying with Madame Charlery, a Martinican from a famous family of traditional musicians, Valérie learned to play ancient island songs. She also developed a strong sense of rhythm, keen memory, and sharp ear. In fact, she learned to play primarily by ear—neither sight-reading nor classical music was a focus of her early education.

And Valérie discovered opera all by herself.

One day she turned on the television to find Verdi's *Aida* on the island's only channel. "It was this huge production. . . . The music was beautiful. . . . We couldn't watch [live] opera in Martinique. We didn't have that. So, it was just magical to see all those people together, being able to play music on the stage."

Valérie had heard her calling. "I just don't know why," she muses, "but I knew I would work in opera."

Martinique has no conservatory to prepare students for a career in classical music. So, after graduating from high school, Valérie set her sights on the Conservatoire de Montpellier in Southern France. She had reservations: "Eighteen years old to go into a conservatory in Europe, in general, is really late. . . . And of course, I didn't have the training." But Valérie had the passion.

She searched high and low for audition pieces and finally found them abroad. "I learned all the music by listening to the recordings, reading a little bit, but *really* listening," Valérie remembers. "And I arrived like that for the audition."

Alas, the music she heard in her head didn't exactly match the sheet music. "I didn't get in because, of course, I wasn't playing exactly what was on the score," Valérie recalls. "I don't know exactly what the jury thought—they probably thought I wasn't taking it seriously!"

Looking back on the experience, Valérie can laugh. But it was a problem at the time—and not just for her. Valérie's parents and two younger brothers had moved to France as well. The Sainte-Agathe family was tight-knit, with mother Armancy, like the many strong women of Martinique, "dealing with everything for the family." Valérie says, "In terms of a leader, she is still an inspiration for me." It was Armancy who had the idea of looking for a piano instructor for Valérie in Montpellier, and sure enough, a member of the conservatory's jury answered the call.

Pianist Jacques Bisciglia had seen something special in Valérie. He gave her a piano lesson every week—sometimes more than one. "We were paying for one hour, and he was always staying longer," she remembers. "During one year, he prepared me to enter the conservatory. . . . It always depends on one teacher."

Valérie's acceptance into the Conservatoire de Montpellier may sound like the end of her challenges, but in fact, those were just beginning.

Suddenly, she found herself among young musicians who'd started training as early as age four. "I felt completely different and isolated at the conservatory because my training wasn't the same [as the other students'separate]," Valérie recalls. "I remember all those pianists playing their scales so fast. And I just couldn't do that." Despite her hard work, there were gaps Valérie couldn't bridge.

But with characteristic resilience, she stuck with the program: "I just ignored everything and just kept following my path. And it's true that I also discovered the strength of my musical training in rhythm. The traditional music [of Martinique] was very important—it helped me a lot, especially working in contemporary music."

At the conservatory, Valérie took a masterclass with conductor René Bosc, who invited her to play an intensely rhythmic piece with the Operá Orchestre national Montpellier (Montpellier National Symphony and Opera). She had no prior experience performing at this level, but it was a success.

And Valérie went on to play and record many other works with René for Radio France. "He was able to see what I could bring to the classical world." She reminds, "It always depends on one teacher."

In classical education, everyone learns the music of the grand masters of piano. This repertoire has been played many times by many excellent musicians. But for Valérie, it was much more interesting to "find a voice" in a new and unheard composition. While those works were not romantic or lyrical enough for many of her peers, Valérie loved modern composers such as John Adams, Steve Reich, and Michael Torke.

By the time Valérie finished her musicology degree at the conservatory, she'd started to consider roles beyond the piano. When an opportunity presented itself during a rehearsal, she jumped at it. "A teacher, a choral conductor, was missing. And I remember they asked me, 'Do you want to lead the rehearsal?' And I just said, 'Well, yes.' And so, I did it. And I just loved it."

Sitting alone at the piano had never come easy to Valérie, but standing in front of a choir did. "It was really natural for me. I didn't know how to do it, but it worked."

The expression "I didn't know how, but . . ." is a catchphrase for Valérie. "Everybody learns in different ways," she explains. "The way I learn is by doing things, is by making mistakes. . . . When you *do* it, you *feel* it also. It's organic, it's embodied."

The Conductor

Conducting is one of the *most* visible but *least* understood jobs in the music world. The short spec is this: a conductor keeps an orchestra or a choir together.

Another way to think of a conductor is as the messenger for the composer, communicating an idea for transforming a score into sound. The seemingly simple gestures they use to do this—waves of a baton or outstretched hand, for example—rely on a complex understanding of musicology, psychology, history, body language, and, of course, sensitivity to the emotions that make us human.

Valérie sums it up like this: "Being a choral conductor is about bringing people together around one idea. It's about believing in each person in the chorus and bringing them up."

Valérie loved this coaching element, and still under the spell of Verdi's enormous *Aida*, she considered moving into orchestral conducting. But she was told that there were no women conductors. "At this time, it was really like that," Valérie admits, "and I didn't even really notice that."

Instead of shying away from conducting altogether, however, she persisted. "What I just decided was, okay, if I can't do it with an orchestra, I'm gonna do it with singers. And this is how it started."

From 1998–2011, Valérie worked at the job she first walked into as a substitute, serving as the music director for the young singers' program at Montpellier National Symphony and Opera. Then, in 2013, while traveling in the United States for an internship, she came across an ad for a music director position with the Grammy Award–winning San Francisco Girls Chorus. Of course, she had to apply.

Valérie returned to France, not really expecting an interview, but the chorus extended an invitation for her to rehearse with the girls.

So, she returned to the United States and aced the audition first time around. Soon after, Valérie moved her own family—a husband and two young daughters—to California.

Though based in San Francisco, the San Francisco Girls Chorus has partnerships across the country.

Valérie conducted the chorus alongside the Knights, a New York–based orchestra, and the Brooklyn Youth Chorus for the NY Philharmonic Biennial at Lincoln Center in 2016.

She made her Carnegie Hall debut in 2018 with the Philip Glass Ensemble, conducting with Michael Riesman in Glass's *Music with Changing Parts*. And in 2019, she performed with the Philip Glass Ensemble again in London at the Barbican Centre.

In early 2020, Valérie's choristers presented the Rightfully Ours concert, featuring two newly commissioned pieces written by female composers Angélica Negrón and Aviya Kopelman.

Valérie seeks out composers, such as these, who think of the child's voice as "an instrument." Contrast that with the idea of simply "writing something for children." The latter can lead to concerns—such as "we need to be careful" and "maybe not too complicated"—which, in turn, can result in less interesting and varied compositions for young voices. "Every subject can be studied and written for children," Valérie insists.

I think girls, in general, have been raised in a way that they—well, *we*—have always had to be pretty, nice, and respectful. And the minute you bring your voice out there, it is often considered as an aggression. . . . By using music, and especially the singing part—because it's really about using the voice—you can build strength and confidence.

Valérie admits that it's not always easy to stand before a group of young women who each have an opinion and want to share it. But she believes "that's what they're supposed to do. They needn't accept 'the way it is' or go along with something because 'you can't change it,' because, in fact, you can."

So, after the Rightfully Ours concert, as news about the COVID-19 crisis circulated in March 2020, Valérie vowed to keep her girls talking and singing and feeling the strength in numbers.

When the Bay Area's shelter-in-place order went into effect, the San Francisco Girls Chorus quickly developed an online program—even before many local schools reopened. They wanted to keep a sense of normalcy, so they kept the same hours and rehearsal times.

Unable to sing together, the girls studied ear training and theory. And early on, when choristers started logging on from their beds, Valérie added choreography—to get the girls moving and learning to use the Zoom window as a stage.

It was hard at first—between the quarantine and the protests against racial injustice, participants had a lot on their minds and hearts. So, discussions about race and equity became part of Valérie's agenda as well. She says, "I took the time to talk to my singers who are African American or mixed race. It's important to make them understand that we are here for them."

Before moving to the United States, Valérie didn't think much about her own racial identity. She simply saw herself as Caribbean, someone connected to Africa, Europe, and—with a great-grandmother in Pondicherry—India. "I think it's only when I arrived here [in the United States] that I actually thought about the fact that I had been the only Black [person at Montpellier Opera]," she admits. "I didn't notice because nobody made me feel that I had to notice. . . . But I felt it here."

As artistic director of the San Francisco Girls Chorus, Valérie focuses on inclusion—bringing young people together around the common goal of music. "If you want them to know what is another culture, another community, and the music from other communities, they need to study, they need to perform it."

Outreach is an important part of Valérie's mission. But she isn't offering short-term assistance—instead, she commits to staying in communities. In 2020, the chorus made the Bayview Opera House an official campus, introducing very young girls to music through chorus prep, chorus essentials, and a full level-one curriculum.

The San Francisco Girls Chorus also commits to in-reach via visits from professional musicians. In 2020, 60 different artists Zoomed in to give masterclasses or cocreate with the choristers. "There is choral music everywhere in the entire world," Valérie says. "And this is what I want to show."

You, too, can see this online at the chorus's website in pieces like "Hallelujah" with the King's Singers and "Music of the Birds" with the Kronos Quartet and *Tomorrow's Memories: A Little Manilla Diary* by Matthew Welch.

These collaborations introduced the choristers to some of the world's finest vocal talent and to the realization that professional artists were suffering through social distancing too. "I think the isolation was really, really difficult to handle," Valérie explains. "For [the girls] to see that there were adult artists who were losing their jobs . . . but they just keep going and wanted to share—that was important."

That's what kept Valérie going—the drive to make music and share music. She didn't know how to conduct a chorus through such challenging times, but (remember that catchphrase mentioned above?) Valérie "learned by doing." And in a time of need, she became "that teacher" for a new generation of young musicians.

Instead of dwindling in size, the San Francisco Girls Chorus grew in 2020–2021 to a 360-girl strong chorus. Its first in-person camp was held in August 2021, nearly a year and a half since the girls were last together at the Rightfully Ours concert. And though the singers were masked, Valérie was thrilled with their performance. "They didn't lose anything," she rejoices, "but they gained a lot."

In the 2021–2022 season, Valérie joined forces with the Grammy Award–winning Kronos Quartet to conduct *At War with Ourselves*, a "beautiful and powerful" piece about African American history, created by composer Michael Abels and poet Nikky Finney. The tour took Valérie across the country, and as the conductor of several different adult choruses, she again enjoyed choral music's strength in numbers.

Remember Valérie's words: "When we are together, we're strong."

Kaoly Asano: Soul, Spirit, and Sound

Look at Kaoly Asano today and you'll see the founder of a free-spirited new style of taiko drumming. She's the lead percussionist of Japan's legendary GOCOO band. With GOCOO, she has performed music for the world's largest festivals and provided music for the sci-fi blockbuster *Matrix Reloaded* and *Matrix Revolutions* movie soundtracks. But on the spring day in 1990 when a friend first invited Kaoly to hit a drum, she was thinking up excuses to stay home.

Kaoly was more than merely disinterested in music—she actively avoided it as a young person. She didn't play an instrument. Ditto for sports. She didn't run, she didn't shout. Laughing and even breathing can be difficult for a child with asthma. The prospect of getting sick was real and frightening. Kaoly had to be careful. She lived a calm and, above all, quiet life.

But out of consideration for her friend, Kaoly accepted the invitation to drum. And that meeting changed everything.

The moment Kaoly stood behind the big barrel-shaped taiko drum, the moment she brought the thick wooden bachi sticks down on the skin, she knew: "I'm finally back where I belong! It was like being struck by a wave of memories that rushed back into my body." She had never played before, yet she could draw sound out of the taiko as if she were drawing on memory.

From then on, Kaoly's life has been anything but quiet.

You may be wondering: *Who is this bold drummer, and what did she do with quiet Kaoly?* It's a good question—one that Kaoly still ponders. "Inside of me, I have two modes," she says, "the ordinary Kaoly Asano and the GOCOO KAOLY."

How did joining a taiko band suddenly tap into all that power? And how does she keep it flowing?

Kaoly was raised in Tokyo and the Kanagawa prefecture in Japan, the most populous metropolitan area in the world. There, she took music classes at an early age, but by second grade, Kaoly had decided that the subject was "very difficult."

That same year she transitioned from public to private school and found herself in a classroom where everyone already understood music theory. Everyone, that is, except Kaoly. She recalls, "Since then, I avoided singing and playing a musical instrument until I met taiko."

Music wasn't the only thing Kaoly missed out on in childhood. Attempts to keep up with the other kids could result in asthma attacks. And worries about physical health affected her mental health. It became a cycle. And to break it, Kaoly broke with Western medicine and took healing into her own hands. Kaoly became a vegetarian. She embraced Eastern medicine. And as a young adult, she studied under a practitioner who taught her about acupuncture—specifically, about how strings of acupuncture points, called the meridian, form a kind of energy superhighway along which Qi (life energy) flows through the body. Using Eastern medicine techniques, Kaoly triggered her own body's healing response and accessed energy reserves that had always eluded her. As her health improved, so did her emotional well-being.

Kaoly came to see that all the years she'd suffered as a youth contained a meaningful lesson: "Whether you are healthy, sick, strong, or weak, one can live the role of his or her life to its fullest." She wanted to share this idea with others.

It seemed natural that Kaoly would go on to treat patients herself, but a seven-year stint as an acupuncturist left her with a "one-way feeling." When she encountered patients resistant to embracing change, Kaoly sensed that she wasn't making enough of a difference. She hadn't found her calling.

During the years before Kaoly discovered taiko, she drifted. "I was choosing to let go of everything and everybody around me," she recalls. "It felt as though another person inside me was making the decisions for me against my will." Perhaps instinct and intuition drove that decision-making. Perhaps it was GOCOO KAOLY.

In the moment Kaoly first hit the taiko, everything she'd learned fell into place.

For example, as an acupuncturist, Kaoly had discovered that the meridian is both the path of Qi and the path of movement, and her unique taiko style draws directly on that insight. The way Kaoly hits the drum doesn't rely on mere muscle power. She explains, "My strike comes from letting the energy from the tanden [the body's center] flow through to the tip of my bachi. Playing taiko this way allows me to feel an endless energy within me."

To understand what she's talking about, pull up a YouTube video from Kaoly's section of the playlist found in the back of this book. Go ahead. The story can wait as you experience the incredible energy of GOCOO.

Taiko

Taiko drums were first beaten thousands of years ago in Japanese villages. Originally made from large hollowed-out tree trunks with cowhide strapped across the tops, the drums make a booming sound when struck, which historians believe served various purposes: it kept time and ordered space (since town boundaries were established by how far the drum was heard from the central square). And for centuries, taiko accompanied dancing in festivals, praying in temples, and fighting in battles.

"Traditional uses were mostly ritualistic and did not use as many drums, drum types, or players as you would see on stage today," Kaoly explains. It wasn't until the second half of the twentieth century, as Japan reaffirmed its identity after World War II, that taiko drumming became a performance art in its own right. In the 1950s, charismatic jazz drummer Daihachi Oguchi established the ensemble taiko style now widely known as "kumi daiko" or simply "taiko."

"Your heart is a taiko," he once told the Associated Press. "All people listen to a taiko rhythm *dontsuku-dontsuku* in their mother's womb. It's instinct to be drawn to taiko drumming."

After Kaoly's life-changing drumming date, her friend became her master, teaching her the essentials such as how to "care for the tone and nuance of the sounds" and "play with the breath." She says, "Everything spirit-wise that a taiko player must nurture, he taught me." But he left the rest to her.

Typically, a member of a taiko group or school would learn the specific form or style of the leader. But Kaoly's master didn't tell her how to hit or what style to play. "I was very lucky that he let me take my time to explore my own path."

Kaoly stayed with her master for six years, until his ensemble disbanded in 1996. This might have been the moment to start a solo career or join a new group—instead, Kaoly rallied the remaining band members and took over as leader.

At that time, it was still common to see all (or mostly) male taiko groups. Taiko was characterized as something "brave" and "masculine," and the women on taiko stages were usually dancing, not drumming.

It seemed as if the only way to "level with men on stage" was to physically train the body and become powerful. But during the 1990s—a period of government investment in regional revitalization—a movement to bring back traditional arts emerged throughout Japan. Community taiko teams formed all over the country, and women joined them.

In 1997, the majority of Kaoly's original band members were female—seven of the twelve. "In the professional taiko field, it was still very rare to have a group led by a woman or a group that featured female performers up front," Kaoly remembers. "For that reason, we attracted a lot of attention."

Kaoly stayed away from all generally accepted notions of taiko: "What I felt with a pure mind when I first started playing taiko was a history much deeper than the history of so-called 'traditional taiko.'" She's referring to a history that stretches all the way back to drumming and dancing at festivals in the primitive era—"the era of the gods."

But Kaoly had no idea whether such a different type of taiko band could "make it."

And then there was the matter of instruments. The band didn't have enough, and taiko are expensive.

Every player needed a set of three to five performance drums, each tuned to a different pitch. Because they consider taiko as their melodic instrument, wind instruments (such as fue) and string (shamisen) were not required. But the ensemble incorporated metal percussion instruments including an atarigane (a hand-held gong played with an antler mallet), a jagan cymbal, and (for occasional use) a slit drum made of bamboo. To make ends meet, the group sought out used instruments and even built their own.

Fortunately, Kaoly enjoyed the sound of secondhand drum skins. She still does. When a drumhead has been played and softened, it creates "deeper, warmer tones that resonate." This is what Kaoly admired about the beat-up 2.5-shaku okedo taiko (an approximately 30-inch diameter staved, roped drum) she picked up for herself. Kaoly says, "To most people it may have looked too worn out, but in my eyes, this taiko looked like an ancient taiko deity and the old skin looked like its universe." Over the years, she has repeatedly sewn the aging, ripped skin.

Kaoly doesn't know how many people played on this drum before it found her, but it's been with her ever since. "To play this taiko means to connect with the person who made the taiko, with the people who have played the taiko, and all the spirits they put into it that becomes the sound."

When Kaoly is on stage with this drum, she feels at peace. "This taiko is my partner and my mentor," she explains. "For this taiko to have found me at the beginning of my life as GOCOO was nothing less than a miracle and a gift from the taiko spirit."

Kaoly gained an opportunity to perform at Japan's first Earth Day event in Tokyo. There, the band attracted the attention of a production team from Rainbow 2000, one of the nation's biggest techno music events. "Not many of us knew what a 'mega outdoor music festival' was like," Kaoly recalls, "but we accepted the performance request without hesitation."

The people who contributed to events like Rainbow 2000 and the now-famous Fuji Rock Festival shared the same ideals—namely, to keep primitive-era festivals alive in the modern world. With the rise of outdoor festivals and raves, people started to recognize new genres such as "roots music" and "world music." And Kaoly is proud that GOCOO was part of that recognition. This shift was a small step toward taiko being seen as "not just a traditional performing art or regional performing art but part of the general music field."

All this validation didn't automatically earn GOCOO a place in traditional music circles, however. Some of those players and afficionados pushed back, claiming, "That is NOT taiko."

That lack of faith would have been undermining without the support of GOCOO's loyal audience. One of the band's steadfast fans encouraged Kaoly with the idea that all traditions start out as something new. Though a new thing is hard to accept, if you don't give up, it will become a tradition.

And sure enough, in 2000, GOCOO was invited to perform at the prestigious Nihon no Taiko (Taiko of Japan) concert held at the National Theatre in Tokyo, the home of Japan's classical performing arts. Kaoly explains, "For GOCOO's taiko to be featured on the opposite ends of the spectrum—on one end at outdoor music festivals and on another end at the Taiko of Japan concert at THE National Theatre—was an unbelievable honor that gave us confidence in what we do."

Another confidence booster: during GOCOO's National Theatre performance, audience members stood up and danced! That behavior is normal for an outdoor festival, but not a Nihon no Taiko concert. Kaoly says, "Culturally, you will never see this happen at a venue like the National Theatre."

GOCOO moved on to the international music scene, playing the huge Sziget Festival in Hungary, the Boom Festival in Portugal, the Montreux Jazz Festival in Switzerland, the Mawazine Festival organized by Morocco's king, and the Festival Internacional Cervantino, the largest international arts festival in Mexico and Latin America. To get an idea of the scale of these shows, see the Paléo Festival Nyon performance in the playlist.

The band represented (musically) the entire Asian continent at the opening event of the UN's Conference on Biological Diversity.

Newsweek Japan featured GOCOO in a special report about "100 Japanese people who overcame cultural barriers and shine in the world," a list of the country's pioneers, heroes, and icons.

Kaoly jokes, "The grade school kid that was traumatized by music would've never imagined a future where music would become her life work that takes her all over the world." And the child who once struggled to keep up with her peers has shared the stage with many highly acclaimed musicians, including famed Korean samul nori player Kim Duk-soo, Seiichi Tanaka, founder of the San Francisco Taiko Dojo, and the late West African djembe player Mamady Keïta. Kaoly toured the United States with the late Native American activist Dennis Banks. And with Juno Reactor, GOCOO recorded music for the *Matrix* movies, which earned more than $1.6 billion worldwide.

The Soul and Spirit in the Sound

The two great inspirations of Kaoly's life are the late Mamady Keïta and the late Dennis Banks. Neither man played Japanese drums, but they helped her "grow an unshakeable root" as a taiko player.

Djembe artist Mamady Keïta founded the renowned Tam Tam Mandingue school of drumming in the West African nation of Guinea before taking his teachings around the world. He also performed and recorded percussion with his group Sewa Kan.

Multitalented Dennis Banks taught, wrote, acted in Hollywood, collaborated with Grammy Award–winning Japanese composer Kitaro on *Let Mother Earth Speak*, and served as a leader in the American Indian Movement.

"These two incredible individuals taught me how to be," Kaoly says. "It's not about what techniques you use or what pieces you perform. It's about whether or not your soul and spirit are in the sound."

Something that has fascinated Kaoly throughout her long career is how to be yourself on stage. When performing, she strives to let go of ego and become a medium of sound. "When there is ego, to try to play better or to try to look good, 100 percent of the time, I will make a mistake, or the performance will not go well," she says. "With a pure and blank mind, I entrust my body, and something lets me play taiko."

Though Kaoly's inner drummer appeared suddenly and unleashed a huge reserve of creative energy, keeping it flowing requires ongoing attention. And that focus wasn't possible during the COVID-19 pandemic.

Right after Kaoly's birthday on March 17, 2020, Japan's social distancing measures forced her to stop playing and performing for the first time in more than 30 years. "I couldn't believe how physically weak I became during that period," she recalls. "I couldn't find any sign of GOCOO KAOLY within me, and I worried that I might have lost her."

But once she was allowed to reopen her dojo, her inner drummer emerged little by little. And when it was time to perform for an audience again, Kaoly took her place behind her favorite okedo taiko. She brought the bachi down on the drumhead. And GOCOO KAOLY exploded back to life.

"I felt an enormous amount of energy burst out as if she could break out of my skin," Kaoly rejoiced. "That energy does not come from me, but it comes as a result of the infinite circulation that occurs by being connected to the audience." That's the key—listeners. Every time, right up to the moment of a performance, Kaoly is nervous, but on stage, all the insecurities disappear and GOCOO KAOLY takes charge.

These distinct aspects of self are important. Kaoly insists, "Only because [Kaoly] knows of her weakness and incompleteness, GOCOO KAOLY will always do her best."

The ability to play taiko that "fell upon" Kaoly, the early discovery of her GOCOO family—these feel like "the work of a miracle." Kaoly says, "This miracle will stay as long as I stay sincere toward taiko. If I slack off or cut corners, the magic will disappear at once. That is a promise I made with the taiko deity."

By playing as GOCOO and operating her own Tokyo dojo, TAWOO, Kaoly is answering a question asked long ago— namely, how to help people live fully. Instead of treating patients, she takes a taiko approach to serving the world. "By delivering a performance or opening a dojo where many people can gather and play taiko easily and in a fun way, I am able to help many people be in touch with their inner energy, filled with love, and exert their own natural healing power."

If you're ever in Tokyo, Kaoly welcomes you to TAWOO.

Part III
Power to Compose

Nami Melumad: Cinematic Scoring

Film composer Nami Melumad's phone buzzed. It was her agent, Maria, calling with a new project.

"There's a spotting session tomorrow, and you're going," said Maria. "You're scoring an episode of *Star Trek: Short Treks.*"

A lifelong Trekkie, Nami gazed at her miniature starship *Enterprise* figurine while the *Star Trek* theme played in her head. This was a dream come true.

What Is a Spotting Session?

Film music heightens emotion, helps with pacing, and sets a tone—for example, tender, sad, eerie, suspenseful, confused, or comedic. During a spotting session, a composer sits with a film director, TV producer, or show runner to "spot" the film scene by scene and discuss how the music will work its magic. The composer and director also determine where each music cue will begin and end.

The next day, Nami met the show's producer, Alex Kurtzman. Together, they watched the episode (titled "Q&A") in which young Ensign Spock, on his first day aboard the USS *Enterprise*, gets trapped in the turbolift (a rapid transport device) with the ship's first officer. Every few seconds they stopped the playback to discuss how the music might best underscore the characters' reactions.

Alex explained what he wanted musically, and Nami boldly offered her own ideas. By the end of the meeting, she had a detailed road map for composing the score. That map would take her where no woman had gone before.

But how did a girl from Israel become a film composer in Hollywood, anyway? It's a tale worthy of its own soundtrack.

Born in 1988, Nami grew up in Ramat Gan (an upper-middle-class Tel Aviv suburb) in a loving, two-parent household, with her older sister Oshrat. Her Israeli father, Meir, managed a pharmaceutical manufacturing plant. Her mother, Aliza, a pharmacist, is Dutch Israeli, so the family also lived in the Netherlands for part of each year.

Nami's other access to the world outside Ramat Gan was through books. Reading the Anne of Green Gables book series, she found a kindred spirit in strong-willed Anne and marveled at nineteenth-century country life in northeast Canada. Reading fantasy series like Harry Potter and Ender's Game, she connected with courageous characters tasked with doing the impossible.

In an effort to understand her own family, Nami read real-life stories of Holocaust survivors and victims, like teen diarist Anne Frank. During the Nazi occupation of the Netherlands, several members of Nami's family were forcibly deported to Nazi concentration camps. Ultimately, her great-grandfather died in Bergen-Belsen, the disease-ridden concentration camp where Anne and her sister Margot also died.

All these stories helped shape Nami's ability to understand the emotions of others. This emotional intelligence would serve her well as a composer.

What shaped her daily life early on, though, was being a little sister. When Oshrat joined the Girl Scouts, Nami joined. When Oshrat swooned over the Backstreet Boys, Nami swooned. When Oshrat started playing piano, Nami played.

But when Oshrat quit piano, Nami kept playing.

Being a musician soon became the one area where Nami was not known as Oshrat's little sister. "I was just me," she says.

In elementary school, nine-year-old Nami developed a crush on a boy who played the euphonium, so she joined the school orchestra. It consisted only of woodwinds (such as flute, oboe, saxophone) and percussion instruments (such as drums, timpani, cymbals). The band teacher assigned Nami the oboe.

To produce sound, the oboist blows into a tiny hole fashioned from two bamboo reeds tied together. It's "a really hard instrument . . . completely insane to study," she says, adding that she was probably picked because she was "stubborn enough to continue."

Nami stuck with the oboe for two years. However, the posture needed to play resulted in tension in her hands, arms, and shoulders, which was very uncomfortable. Nami's mom was unwilling to keep watching her daughter struggle, and she suggested Nami switch to flute which required a more open, "less squeezed" posture.

"It will open up your world," she predicted. And it did. Nami fell in love with the flute.

Like her parents, she was also passionate about science. She excelled in STEM classes and considered a career in technology, chemistry, or medicine.

However, Nami did not share her parents' interest in classical music, and she often slept through the second half of the classical concerts her family attended. She preferred pop music: Britney Spears, NYSNC, and her beloved Backstreet Boys.

Then, in middle school, film music captured her imagination. Obsessed with John Williams's score to *Home Alone* (1990) and Fons Merkies's score to *Twin Sisters* (a 2002 Dutch film set during World War II), she tried playing them on piano. That's when she realized that she could play anything if she broke it down into harmony (chords) and melody.

In eighth grade, Nami asked her "cool" cousin Ido Birger to teach her guitar. He gave her a few lessons, then turned her loose with a book to learn chord structures.

"Understanding about chord progressions enabled me to start thinking of my own little stuff," she says. Soon she was writing melodies.

At 14, Nami's film music obsession was the Lord of the Rings trilogy. She not only taught herself to play the score, but she also started composing music for an imaginary fourth installment of the series, just for fun. "With film music," she says, "you could write music and you could tell a story too."

After high school, Nami began a two-year stint in the Israeli Defense Forces (IDF), mandatory for all Israelis regardless of gender. She served in a noncombat position as an interviewer at a recruiting office. Her job was to listen compassionately and gain the recruits' trust so she could help them navigate the choices ahead.

Nami never missed a day. Having grown up in a suburban "bubble," she was meeting people from socioeconomic and cultural backgrounds outside her experience, and their stories fascinated her.

Some were worried about how their gender identity or sexual preference might impact their military service. Those were concerns Nami could relate to. She was dating a man (the euphonium player from elementary school), but she was also attracted to a female friend in the IDF.

Watching American films and television shows with LGBTQIA+ characters, like *The L Word*, helped her to work out her own sexual identity. Nami soon realized that she was bisexual, and when she came out to her parents, they were loving and supportive.

After finishing her IDF service, Nami took a job in a restaurant, saving money for a trip around the world. Every day in the restaurant, as the same boring tunes played over and over, she wondered what the soundtrack to her future would be. Would the playlist in a medical lab or tech company be this bad? *Probably.* Nami crossed those careers off her list.

Meanwhile, she listened to the soundtracks she loved while driving her car. One day, a friend who was riding and listening along, asked, "Which movie is this from?"

Movie?

"I wrote this," Nami replied.

It was her "Lord of the Rings 4" music.

"Wow!" said her friend.

Nami decided then and there to apply to the Jerusalem Academy of Music and Dance.

But first, she took the trips she'd been saving for—a "small backpack trip" around Israel, Europe, Canada, and the United States and a "big backpack trip" to Australia and New Zealand. As a Lord of the Rings geek, she planned her New Zealand trek around film locations. It was thrilling.

Back home, Nami aced the Jerusalem Academy of Music and Dance entrance exam and audition. Impressed, the jury invited her to enter the academy as a sophomore as long as she read all the first-year textbooks over the summer.

Come fall, Nami dove into her interdisciplinary composition studies. She had multiple ideas for most of her assignments. "When I'm interested in something," she says, "I become a true nerd. So I would submit two versions of everything."

The academy's only film-scoring classes were for master's degree students, but Nami asked to audit them. Auditors receive no college credit for their work, but Nami still completed every assignment.

That uncredited work soon paid off. Upon graduation from the academy, Nami was accepted to the prestigious scoring for motion pictures and TV graduate certificate program at the University of Southern California (USC) in L.A.

During the nine-month gap between schools, she taught music to children. She also volunteered at the Tel Aviv Municipal LGBTQ Center teaching music to displaced youth sheltering there. For the first time, she felt at home within the larger LGBTQIA+ community.

When at last she moved to L.A., she found herself in a whole different world from Ramat Gan.

One big surprise was the huge gender gap in the Hollywood film music industry. Nami had winced at the lack of female professors at the academy but hadn't realized this was the norm. When she'd studied composer Rachel Portman's film music, no one had mentioned that Rachel was an exception in a male-dominated field. In hindsight, she's actually glad she didn't know there were so few women because, she explains, "I never felt as if I didn't have a chance."

She says, "You get in a room and the engineer is a guy, the arranger is a guy, the composer, if there's a composer, is a guy, the conductor is a guy, the contractor is a guy. This is the team that you see all the time." Regardless of the imbalance, Nami has never been treated with disrespect by anyone in the studio.

And the Oscar Goes to . . .

British composer Rachel Portman was the first female composer to win an Academy Award. She won for *Emma*, a 1996 film starring Gwyneth Paltrow. She was also the first woman to win a Primetime Emmy Award, for her score for *Bessie*—a 2015 TV movie starring Queen Latifah as Blues legend Bessie Smith. She received additional Academy Award nominations for *The Cider House Rules* (1999) and *Chocolat* (2000)—scores Nami listened to as a kid and studied in college.

Rachel, who has scored over 100 film, television, and theatrical productions, says, "I'm always fascinated by the alchemy of putting music against the moving image. There's a big part of me that enjoys dramatizing and is interested in defining emotions and then being able to express them—but very specific ones." Like Nami, she considers herself "a storyteller."

Nami also admires film scores by German composer Anne-Kathrin Dern, Irish composer Amie Doherty,

Academy Award-winning British composer Anne Dudley (*The Full Monty*), and Academy Award-winning Icelandic composer Hildur Guðnadóttir (*The Joker*), to name a few.

At USC, Nami was paired with a mentor: 15-time Academy Award–nominated composer Thomas Newman (*The Shawshank Redemption, American Beauty, Finding Nemo, WALL-E*). He invited her to work sessions at his studio and to the *Finding Dory* recording session at Fox's famed Newman Scoring Stage. She can't imagine a better mentor than Tom.

Nami took advantage of every opportunity at USC. At a student mixer, she connected with USC School of Cinematic Arts (SCA) graduate students who needed music for their film projects. Only SCA students could use the John Williams Scoring Stage at USC, and Nami wanted to record on that stage. In one year's time she composed and recorded scores for 15 SCA student films.

One of those student films was animator Catherine Chooljian's *Luminarias*, a five-minute short in which a grieving child follows a magic jellyfish skyward to convene with her mama's spirit. In 2017, it won Best Score at Fimucite, the Tenerife International Film Music Festival. Watch it on Vimeo.

Fresh out of USC, Nami concentrated on scoring independent features, shorts, and documentaries. She volunteered with Women in Film and also joined OutFest, which provides visibility to LGBTQIA+ stories and storytellers. Through these two organizations, Nami met filmmakers who care about what she cares about, and she got work.

She wouldn't take just any project though, something about it had to call to her. "It's the director, it's the characters, it's the type of music that I maybe didn't work in before. So it gave me a new canvas or a challenge," she recalls.

She also enjoyed working with small budgets because it pushed her to be highly creative. "You have no budget, but you still make something amazing and great."

Those independent film scores got noticed. Nami won a Hollywood Music in Media Award (HMMA) for scoring *Passage* (2018), a 20-minute short film about the relationship between mothers and daughters. She was also nominated for HMMAs for her scores for *This Day Forward* (2017) and *Miss Arizona* (2018). And her score for *Over the Wall* (2019), a short film about the friendship between two boys—one Israeli, the other Palestinian—earned her a Jerry Goldsmith Award nomination.

Nami has a huge reservoir of compassion, and she does what it takes to connect with characters outside her experience. She scored *Subira* (Kenya's 2018 Oscar entry), a feature film about a young Muslim woman's choice to defy gender stereotypes; *More Beautiful for Having Been Broken* (2019), a feature film about a single mother with a child that has special needs; and the documentary *Not Your Skin* (2019), an intimate look at four transgender individuals in transition.

Small projects led to bigger projects because people remembered the quality of her work. A film editor, who she worked with on the short thriller *Mindgame*, recommended her for the Amazon thriller series *Absentia*.

In November 2018, at the suggestion of her agent Maria, Nami made a pitch to compose music for the HBO Max feature film *An American Pickle* starring Seth Rogen. "Rogen plays both Hershel—a Jewish immigrant who is accidentally pickled inside a factory for 100 years—and his great-grandson Ben, who he meets when he wakes up."

Maria called Nami about *Pickle* on a Friday. A sample reel was due on Monday. "So I wrote some stuff—and luckily I also had some stuff from previous projects that fit that description—and I had my cousin [Ran Kampel] record some clarinet on his iPhone," she says.

Four weeks later, Maria called with Oscar-winning composer Michael Giacchino *(Up, Star Trek, Coco, Cars)* on the line. He invited Nami to score *Pickle*.

Michael and Nami spotted the film together, and Nami learned a great deal "from his incredible understanding of the story" and how he "relates to the picture."

Michael wrote the basic themes, and Nami's job was to turn four and a half minutes of theme music into 60-plus minutes of score. It was a huge challenge, but she "figured it out." Her Jewish heritage and familiarity with Eastern European melodies further helped her to align the score with the story. That score earned Nami a 2020 International Film Music Critics

Association (IFMCA) nomination for Best Score for a Comedy Film.

Michael also helped Nami break into another arena: video games. Knowing what she could do with his themes, he invited her to score *Medal of Honor: Above and Beyond*, the sequel to *Medal of Honor*, which he scored in 1999.

To get the combatants' perspective, Nami read firsthand accounts of World War II veterans. This helped her to imagine what the player/soldier was experiencing in various game scenarios and to match the heightened emotion of those scenes musically.

The score for *Medal of Honor: Above and Beyond* was recorded at London's famous Abbey Road Studios with what Nami calls "one of the best orchestras in the world." However, because the sessions took place during the height of the COVID-19 pandemic, Nami participated remotely. Even from afar, the musicians' performances took her breath away. And she wasn't the only one.

In 2020, Nami's score for *Medal* won the IFMCA award for Best Original Score for a Video Game. She also garnered a 2020 IFMCA Breakthrough Composer of the Year Nomination (for *Medal* and *Pickle* combined).

The video game also features short documentaries—stories of heroism during World War II—which Nami scored. *Colette*, the longest, is about a teenage member of the French resistance whose older brother died at age 19 in the Mittelbau-Dora concentration camp in Germany. In the film, Colette, now 90, journeys to Mittelbau-Dora to honor her brother.

Aware of her own family's losses, Nami put her heart into this project, and her deeply moving score won a 2021 BMI Film & Music Award. Of course, Nami was thrilled when *Colette* won the 2021 Academy Award for Best Documentary Short Subject.

In 2021, Nami composed the score for Disney's short film *Far from the Tree*. She scored the 2022 Netflix series *The Woman in the House Across the Street from the Girl in the Window*.

In 2022, Nami also joined the Marvel universe, cocomposing with Michael Giacchino for the feature film *Thor: Love and Thunder*.

And remember Nami's 2019 *Star Trek: Short Treks* episode, "Q&A"? Her work so impressed producers that they signed her to score not one but two *Star Trek* series: the *Star Trek: Prodigy* animated series and the *Star Trek: Strange New Worlds* live action series, both of which launched in 2022. This makes Nami the first female composer to score an entire *Star Trek* series or movie.

To paraphrase the opening lines of the original 1966–1969 *Star Trek* series, Nami Melumad is boldly going where no woman has gone before.

Joanne Shenandoah: Standing in Power

Ms. Shenandoah was considered the matriarch of Indigenous music.

—*New York Times*

She was not only exceptionally beautiful but gracious, remarkably talented and blessed with natural charisma; she was also given to marvelous laughter.

—Doug George-Kanentiio,
Akwesasne Mohawk journalist/historian
and Joanne's husband

Glowing and heartfelt tributes such as these circulated in the media after Joanne Shenandoah passed away on November 22, 2021. In this chapter, *Music Mavens* pays homage to the legendary musician, drawing on a treasured interview conducted with her in June 2021.

Joanne grew up on the Oneida Iroquois Territory in upstate New York. The Shenandoah home lacked running water, but it was full of music—the jazz of Duke Ellington and Billie Holiday and the country songs of Hank Williams and Patsy Cline.

As a child, Joanne learned this music as well as all the tribal songs. "My family always taught me to be proud that I was an Iroquois woman and the importance of what our culture had to offer us," she remembered.

She loved the singing societies of Iroquois women. In the Iroquois tradition, it's the women—the matriarchs and the clan mothers—who are responsible for the political, social, and spiritual welfare of the people. "They taught the young men their songs."

For Joanne, music was an integral part of self and society. "Every word we speak; every song we sing; the songs which we subject ourselves to, whether in the womb, or as an elder, these songs affect us in very powerful and meaning[ful] ways," she said. "They can actually help to destroy us, or they can help to heal us."

Singing came as easy to Joanne as breathing, and she was a natural-born instrumentalist. Her mother once remarked, "What amazed me when she was young, she could just pick up any instrument and start playing it."

Joanne's affinity for music is reflected in her Native name, Tekaliwhakwah. Given to her as a little girl by a visionary, the name combines two elements that translate to "She Sings" and "Lifting the Spirit." It's a unique name. No one else has it. And the idea it carries—of musical ambassadorship—is both a gift and a responsibility.

The spotlight settled on Joanne early, but stage shows weren't easy at first. She remembered her parents coaxing her to perform at a concert in third grade. (Though she didn't feel like going, she couldn't get out of it.) And to Joanne's surprise, she won the grand prize in front of several generations of family. "My grandma was there—it was really beautiful."

A teen in the 1970s, Joanne looked up to well-known Native American musicians such as Rita Coolidge, Buffy Sainte-Marie, A. Paul Ortega, Jim Pepper, Floyd Westerman, and the rock bands Redbone and XIT. But there were still relatively few Indigenous artists in mainstream music. And the National Academy of Recording Arts and Sciences would not offer a Grammy Award for Best Native American Music Album for several decades.

At age 15, Joanne left home to attend boarding school at Union Springs Academy in Union Springs, New York. She was the only Native American student there, and she dove into music. "I grabbed the books that show you how to play the music and did it myself," Joanne remembered. "It was so fun for me to just try out everything." She learned French horn, cello, clarinet, and flute. She spent hours practicing piano and learning to read and write music. She developed her singing and composition skills, writing songs ranging from solo pieces to full symphonies.

Joanne loved stretching her wings. But at the end of her education—when it came time to fly—she did not rise on a musical updraft. And she didn't glide home. Instead, Joanne moved to the Washington, DC, area to start a corporate job.

Putting aside her musical aspirations, Joanne took her knowledge of business administration—acquired at Andrews University in Berrien Springs, Michigan, and Montgomery College in Maryland—and went to work in computer consulting. She explained, "I guess I just needed to find a way to make money." And Joanne made a lot of it managing a large team. "I was working very hard and was doing all the things I thought were important in life," she remembered. But something was missing.

After more than a decade of desk work, Joanne suddenly saw it: While gazing out an office window one day in 1990, she spotted a massive oak tree being taken down. "It just uprooted me," she said. In that moment, Joanne realized that just as the tree had been torn from its place in the ground, she, too, had been removed from her homeland:

> I knew I had to go back to where my ancestors once lived, where they sang their songs, where they danced their dances. And I knew at that point I needed to have the place where they prayed, the place where they lived, the place

where they died. The place that would offer me everything I needed to have in order to fulfill my destiny—which is music. And given that my name is Tekaliwhakwah, this is something that was meant to be.

Once Joanne committed to life as a musician, she didn't look back.

Living in Oneida territory, she sought out elders to learn more about the history and languages of her people and other groups in the Iroquois Confederacy.

Joanne also met Doug George-Kanentiio, the Akwesasne Mohawk journalist and historian who would become her husband. He'd been invited to her home by matchmakers to see if there was an attraction. "There was," Doug recalls, "as soon as Jo entered the room, I knew with certainty we would marry but she did not." It took a visit to a seer to convince Joanne, but the couple soon wed and went on to make history together.

When Joanne's music career began, her songs and stories were efforts to transform the hundreds of years of marginalization of First Nations peoples. Longtime friend and fellow musician Marisa Arbona-Ruiz explains, "Every breath she took, every song she sang was her way of saying, 'HERE WE ARE.'"

Joanne's voice is an expression of what the Iroquois refer to as "the good mind," says Native American studies scholar Christopher Vecsey. "Her voice never stretches. It never goes to edges. It's always right in the center, beautifully calm." Singer-songwriter Robbie Robertson intones, "She weaves you into a trance with her beautiful Iroquois chants and wraps her voice around you like a warm blanket on a cool winter's night."

You've probably felt the comfort of that blanket—perhaps without even knowing whom to thank—because Joanne's voice can be heard everywhere.

Her voice, singing or speaking, has been featured in hundreds of commercials, children's stories, and films. You can hear her in the television program *Northern Exposure* and the film *Indian in the Cupboard*, documentaries like Discovery Channel's *How the West Was Lost*, and PBS specials, including the award-winning *Warrior in Two Worlds*.

An intuitive artist, Joanne could perform live shows without following a setlist and preferred to let creative juices flow in the studio (rather than planning out every recording detail). And whenever Joanne needed a new song, she simply sat down and wrote one.

She didn't use tricks to coax the creative muse. But neither did she take personal credit for her songs—they were all ancestrally inspired. "When I create music," Joanne explained, "I'm coming from a place that is purely a vessel. . . . I've asked for it, and I'm there."

Joanne's music covered the spectrum from traditional and folk to Americana, country, pop, and even New Age, performed in both English and her native language. Iroquois influences were ever-present in her music.

You can hear them in the following five *Music Mavens* favorites chosen from her enormous discography of nearly 500 songs.

"Kahawi'tha," on the *Matriarch* album, is a collection of Iroquois women's melodies and chants recorded at ancient village sites on the Oneida territory in New York.

"Prophecy Song" is a sacred piece performed for the Parliament of the World's Religions and many other audiences. Joanne and her daughter, Leah Shenandoah, sing it a cappella in a gorgeous recording for the *Global Spirit* episode "Music, Sound, and the Sacred." Listen to the short conversation that follows in which Joanne explains the song's ability to speak to people across language barriers.

"Skywoman" is a pop-orchestral production of an Iroquois creation story that tells how Skywoman falls from the upper world and how the animals living in the watery place below catch her and create a ground for her to stand on. A favorite of Joanne's, the idea came from a book she coauthored with Doug.

"Treaty," on the album *Eagle Cries*, won Joanne a Nammy Artist of the Year award in 2002. Written with Brian Fitzpatrick and Neil Young, the song addresses the treatment of Native Americans by federal authorities.

"Seeking Light" is Joanne's solo track on *Sacred Ground: A Tribute to Mother Earth*, a compilation album showcasing the creativity and diversity of Indigenous artists. It won a Grammy Award for Best Native American Music Album in 2006.

For the Love of Music

Joanne shared the stage and studio with countless celebrities, but she credited her parents as her greatest musical influences. "They nurtured my love for music from the beginning."

Joanne's father, Pine Tree Chief Clifford Schenandoah (some family members spell the name with a "c") of the Onondaga Nation, Beaver Clan, was an iron worker who loved jazz and played guitar with the legendary Duke Ellington.

Through her father's line, Joanne is a direct descendant of famed Chief Skenandoa (also known as John Shenandoah), an ally of George Washington during the American Revolution.

Joanne's mother, Maisie Shenandoah, was an Oneida Wolf Clan Mother who also sang, played guitar, and sold traditional arts. Masie hails from the Oneida Nation of New York, which has a matrilineal kinship system, so Joanne and her four siblings are considered to be born into the Wolf Clan.

Reflecting on what this identity element meant to her music, Joanne said, "These things are very real to me. [They are a form] of living Cultural Survival. If you listen to some of the songs I've written, [you'll see that] I do howl a lot about a lot of issues. I'm in the forefront when someone asks me to [sing] at a major event. It's a very conscious sort of music, very healing I think."

In a career spanning more than three decades, Joanne earned 40-plus music awards, including a Grammy, 14 Nammys (the most Native American Music Awards earned by any individual), and a Lifetime Legend Award by the American Indian Society. Ever humble, Joanne said, "Winning and bringing the trophy home is not so important as hoping people will get my message. Mine is a message of peace, not only for the Iroquois community, but for everyone."

Joanne performed at the White House (for five US presidential inaugurations), the Parliament of the World's Religions, and Saint Peter's Basilica in the Vatican for the canonization of the first Native American saint, Saint Kateri Tekakwitha.

She traveled the world to meet leaders such as His Holiness the Dalai Lama, Nelson Mandela, and former Russian president Mikhail Gorbachev.

She served as cochair, with US Attorney General Eric Holder, for the Task Force on American Indian and Alaska Native Children Exposed to Violence during the Obama administration.

And among her most important legacy projects is the Hiawatha Institute for Indigenous Knowledge, a nonprofit, higher-learning facility that provides all nations and peoples with access to the ancient teachings and peace principles of the Haudenosaunee (Iroquois).

When asked about the challenges of professional life—work involving world travel, diplomacy, activism, and the music industry—Joanne pointed to her matriarchal heritage and strong female role models. That's not to say she didn't experience marginalization as a woman and an Indigenous person, but she didn't keep that focus. "[If you] stand in your power, people don't mess with you."

For Joanne, that power came from being rooted in her home and community.

In preparation for her opening of the 2020 Global Awareness Conference, Joanne said, "This is what I do, this is my life. I am Oneida Iroquois of the Wolf Clan, my dad was a chief, my mom was a Clan Mother and primarily my music is my gift to the world."

True to the elder's vision, Tekaliwhakwah lifted spirits with her songs. In the words of her daughter, Leah, "Her light and beauty is eternal. And it will always live on through her music and the people's lives she touched."

Kate Schutt:
Presence Not Perfection

Three themes guide the life and lyrics of guitarist and singer-songwriter Kate Schutt: "presence not perfection," "all in with pluck and zeal," and "being enough."

Kate lives by these words—words that have been hard earned.

When her mother was diagnosed with cancer, Kate became her full-time caregiver. For nearly five years she caused herself to be present, all in, enough.

As she lived this horrible, rotten, sometimes achingly beautiful, and often terrifying experience, Kate kept a notebook. Out of that notebook came *Bright Nowhere*, an album that bravely looks death in the eye and melts listeners' hearts. In "You More Than Me," she sings:

I can't imagine how you must feel
Though I try to put myself in your place
I press my heart to your heart
My face to your face
The unbroken expanse
The unbridgeable space

Kate Schutt was born in 1975 in Chadds Ford, Pennsylvania, a rural town just north of Wilmington, Delaware. Her father, Chip, worked in finance, and her mother, Katharine, was a mom, school board trustee, and community volunteer.

Kate spent her childhood keeping up with older brothers, Jake and Porter. She was a woodsy girl, most comfortable in jeans and work boots. In winter, her favorite season, she ice skated and played pond hockey at her grandmother's farm and was (still is!) "a sledding fool." In grade school, she played field hockey, ice hockey, and lacrosse.

She loved making visual art. Among childhood art pieces saved by her mom is a collaged cardboard car Kate created, above which she scribbled, "Art is the most fantastic!" Even then, there were clues as to what she'd end up doing.

Records often played on the family stereo in the Schutt house. Her parents' favorite was *Ella Fitzgerald Sings the Cole Porter Songbook*. They played it repeatedly, and Ella's singing and Cole's songwriting had a lasting impact on Kate.

Musical talent ran on her father Chip's side of the family. Her grandmother and three aunts all played the piano, and Chip played the harmonica perfectly with zero lessons.

Kate's brothers, seemingly, expressed no interest in playing. So, determined to turn out at least one musician, her parents started Kate on piano. And though she is grateful for the enforced lessons now, 10-year-old Kate had other ideas.

As she listened to Tina Turner's *Private Dancer* album over and over on her Smurf Walkman, Kate dreamed of playing rock guitar. When she asked for lessons, her mom signed her up for a basic acoustic guitar class at school. Soon, Kate requested an electric guitar and a more serious teacher.

Wilmington-based bebop guitarist John Dougherty agreed to teach Kate under one condition. Before she could start, she had to write an essay titled, "What Is Music?" John would use Kate's essay to gauge her seriousness and examine her thought processes.

Kate remembers sitting on the olive-green shag carpet in her living room searching for words. "I was at a loss," she says. "No one had ever asked me to describe the indescribable."

John accepted her as a jazz guitar student and immediately had her "playing all over the guitar neck." A gifted player and inspiring teacher, John would continue to mentor Kate until his death in 2011.

In middle school, Kate was in a band called the Headley Combs. They played songs by the Grateful Dead, Jimi Hendrix, Janis Joplin, and the Doors, practicing in the lead guitarist's garage. One day, they decided they would try to write an original song. As Kate remembers it, on the garage wall hung "a funky poster that was sort of a line drawing of a guy standing in front of a house." Their first song—"Old Man Winslow"—brought the "poster guy" to life.

Throughout elementary and middle school, Kate played ice hockey on teams with boys. But in high school, the teams were segregated by gender, and there were no high school girls' teams in her area. Kate wanted to play so she started ninth grade at Taft, a Connecticut boarding school with a girls' ice hockey team.

The day her parents dropped her off there, she had a realization: no one at Taft knew her. Up to that point, she'd entered every room as "Porter and Jake's little sister" or "Katharine's daughter." Here, she was free to "define" herself.

This epiphany energized her to excel in academics, the arts, and her beloved sports. She learned Mandarin, began painting, and played in a rock band and an acoustic guitar duo. Self-directed and self-disciplined, Kate was admitted to Harvard University in Boston, Massachusetts.

There, Kate continued to follow her passions. She loved language and reading, creative and analytical writing, and critical thinking—so she majored in English literature. She also played both women's ice hockey and lacrosse. Playing two Division 1 sports and maintaining her grades was a full-time job.

One day, while walking to the ice hockey rink, she calculated the total number of hours she was putting into sports. With games on Wednesdays, Saturdays, and Sundays, practice, weightlifting, physical therapy, and travel, ice hockey consumed from 4 to 24 hours each day. And for what? Kate loved playing, loved her teammates, but she realized there was no future in it.

She asked herself: *What if I took a break from playing sports and devoted that time to guitar?* Maybe she could study at nearby Berklee College of Music. Harvard didn't have a dual degree with Berklee (they do now), but she wondered about taking a leave of absence.

Berklee had no audition process then, so Kate simply filled out the application, submitted her transcripts, and waited. She didn't tell anyone she'd applied—not her teammates, not her coaches, not her parents. When her acceptance letter arrived, she asked her mom and dad if she could study music at Berklee for a year, then finish her degree at Harvard. They said yes.

Kate took her last sophomore exam at Harvard on her first day of summer classes at Berklee. That day she discovered three things:

One, she was the only female student at Berklee studying guitar performance.

Two, there were big gaps in her music education: What was ear training? What was harmonic analysis?

Three, compared to everyone else, she was a terrible player. All those hours Kate had put into her sports, fellow students had put into their instruments and musicianship.

She had work to do. Kate made it her job to be the first person in the practice room when it opened at 7:00 AM and the last one out when it closed at 3:00 AM She was totally focused on improving as fast as she could.

Instead of one year, Kate studied at Berklee, almost year-round, for two solid years. She learned a lot and improved enough to play in some ensembles in her last few semesters. Berklee was intense, and by fall of 1997 she was ready to change things up. So, she returned to Harvard to finish her degree.

She also returned to sports. That year, she was honored with Harvard's John Dooley Award in ice hockey. In lacrosse, she was top goalie in the league and named First-Team All-Ivy. Then she aged out of the NCAA. So, during her senior year, she was Harvard's assistant women's ice hockey coach.

Kate's academic interest was poetry, specifically the work of Pulitzer Prize–winning poet Elizabeth Bishop. Now recognized as one of the best poets of the twentieth century, Bishop disliked being labeled a "female poet" or "lesbian poet," though both applied. While at Harvard, Kate herself came out, but like Bishop, she sees her sexual orientation as a nonstory. "I am who I am; I love who I love," she says.

Kate graduated from Harvard magna cum laude in 1999. After graduation, she turned to writing songs, playing in clubs, touring, recording, and building a fan base.

Then, in 2002, Kate was diagnosed with nodules (noncancerous bumps) on her vocal cords. She underwent surgery, after which she was not allowed to speak. One period of complete vocal rest lasted three months. She only communicated via a whiteboard. Healing was a long, slow process fraught with many setbacks.

But as a result, Kate grew. She learned that she was not defined just by her voice. It was possible for her to fully express herself without it.

Also, because during the vocal rest she couldn't use her voice to match a pitch, her internal sense of pitch (her ability to match a pitch in her head) improved. So did her musicianship. She bought a used four-string electric bass and learned to play it. Then she started playing a hybrid guitar/bass with eight strings.

Aware that many individuals have lifelong difficulty producing oral speech, Kate was grateful when her speaking and singing voice healed completely. In 2003, she moved to Canada and began performing and touring again. She recorded an album of five jazz/pop songs titled *Heart-Shot* (2004) on which she played the eight-string. Two cowritten, self-produced, full-length albums followed: *No Love Lost* (2007), which topped the Canadian jazz charts, and *The Telephone Game* (2009).

Kate's song, "How Much in Love?" (cowritten with Jesse Ruddock) won the 2007 John Lennon Songwriting Contest for Jazz. In 2009, her song "Take Me with You" (also cowritten with Jesse) was one of four finalists in the same category.

In 2010, she relocated to Manhattan to be at the center of the jazz world.

"Then in 2011, I got the gig that every musician wants to get at some point," Kate recalls. It was a long-term contract to play at a hotel in Qatar. For the coming months, she'd be able to "woodshed"—have a steady, well-paying gig, where she could work on her playing and musicianship day in and day out.

Kate packed her bags and took a train home to say goodbye to her parents. When she arrived, her mom confessed she'd been unwell and was awaiting CT scan results.

The scan revealed a tumor in her abdomen.

Kate's mother had a rare, incurable form of ovarian cancer.

Kate canceled her contract in Qatar, put her guitar in a corner of her childhood bedroom, and set out to help her mother through her treatment. For the first year and a half of that journey, she didn't touch her guitar. She took her mother to doctor appointments, held her hand through every bad news conversation, made her meals, and supported her through a host of brutal procedures all designed to delay the inevitable.

Kate kept a notebook with her at all times and would jot down thoughts, experiences, words, phrases. And although she had no time for songwriting, she challenged herself to capture 10 song ideas a day. After a year, she had filled three notebooks.

In March 2013, her mother went into remission, and Kate headed to Wyoming with her notebooks for a six-week artist residency at the Ucross Foundation. Ucross typically serves artists who are farther along in their careers, and Kate was humbled and surprised to be granted a coveted slot.

Those six weeks, in a beautiful cabin with a grand piano, changed Kate's life. Unsure she'd remember how to write one song, Kate wrote five. While there, she also met and fell in love with her partner, Leah.

The first song to emerge was "Death Come Slow." "I had a few things I needed to say to the figure of Death that was now hanging around, casting a shadow," she says.

> Death come slow
> Death come shy
> Death don't you look her in the eye

She also had things to say to her mother, who'd often expressed that she felt like a burden to her family and friends. How could Kate convince her otherwise? Maybe the way in was through music.

When she returned home, Kate recorded a demo version of "Nothing I Won't Bear" and played it for her mom.

> I know you are weary
> I know you are scared
> There's nothing I won't do for you
> There's nothing I won't bear

Katharine listened to the song over and over.

"It was as if my song—or the act of me writing the song—lowered the volume on her private anguish," Kate recalls. "Going forward, I noticed she was able to let more love in, all the love that was coming from beyond the immediate family and her closest friends."

Kate's mom "lived full out" for four and a half years. On October 13, 2015, she died.

Afterward, Kate remained at home, helping her dad get his bearings. When at last she returned to New York, she'd been gone for five years.

Kate started a business—Incandescent Coaching—to "help top-performers rise above the plateaus that keep them from their full potential." The income allowed her to continue transforming her heartbreak into healing art.

Unsure if she had the makings of an album or if her "death songs" would work in concert, Kate tried them with live audiences. Cancer patients, survivors, caregivers, and people who'd experienced loss, connected deeply with her music. "They just really recognized their journey in it—the bittersweetness, the toughness of all their decisions."

The new songs were more Americana flavored than jazz influenced. When asked about crossing genres, Kate says, "I always go where the song leads me. The song comes first; it has to. . . . Genre is never a consideration."

For years, Kate lived with the songs that would end up on *Bright Nowhere*. When friends suggested spare arrangements for the album—just vocals and guitar—she balked. Her vision included a bigger sound. However, she knew the material was "too close to the bone" for it to be self-produced. So, she started inquiring about potential producers, and her publisher suggested Rob Mounsey.

A six-time Grammy nominee and two-time Emmy winner, Rob had produced albums for dozens of big-name artists. "He had the chops and the network to take my vision and make it bigger, grander, more cinematic," she says.

Kate called Rob and they spent time together talking about life and loss. She asked him if he'd consider producing the album, and he said yes.

When they discussed who she wanted on the team, Kate chose to enlist top-tier people, adding thousands of dollars to her budget. She was self-funding the album, so she coached and coached to make the money to pay these dream musicians.

Before each recording session began, Kate asked the players, backing vocalists, and engineers to share about people they'd loved and lost. Photos of their loved ones graced the studio, and everyone became deeply invested in the project.

The 13-song album *Bright Nowhere* was released in 2021 to critical acclaim. *Americana Highways* reviewer John Apice called it "one of the year's best." He wrote, "It possesses a Billie Holiday mystique. It has an intensity that can hold an audience's attention with its haunting vocal, chilling yet warm simultaneously. Kate is superb."

The album, best listened to straight through, is not all darkness. A lot of light shines through too, especially on Kate's up-tempo tracks. For those who've lost someone—a friend, a family member, even a beloved pet—Kate's songs can serve as "a kind of key for the lock of loss." In fact, they helped Kate through her next round with grief when her dad died in 2021.

Kate approaches everything she does—composing, coaching, performing, producing, practicing, writing, public speaking, volunteering—with a simple goal: presence not perfection.

She gave a TEDx Talk (available on YouTube) titled *Grief Casserole—How to Help Your Friends and Family Through Loss*, where she shares, vulnerably, about caring for and losing her mother, sings snippets of her songs a cappella, and leaves listeners with simple but powerful advice on how to support someone who is dealing with death.

Kate is now writing songs for her next album, and you can follow the process on her blog at kateschutt.com.

Want to get to know Kate personally? Participate in her "Mail Me 1 Thing" project. Mail her one thing and she'll mail you one thing back. You'll find the details on her website.

Writing letters by hand is part of her creative process. And who knows? Maybe your "1 Thing" will inspire a song.

Kate's Faves

Favorite female singers: Ella Fitzgerald, Aretha Franklin, Tina Turner, Nina Simone, Sarah Vaughan (aka "Sassy"), and Cassandra Wilson

Favorite drummer: Terri Lyne Carrington

Dream project: Having Diana Krall or Cassandra Wilson sing one of her songs

Artists she'd like you to meet: Camille O'Sullivan, Lori Cullen, and the Good Lovelies

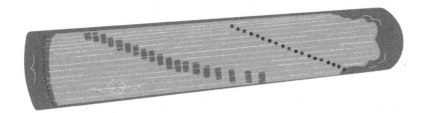

Part IV
Power to Improvise

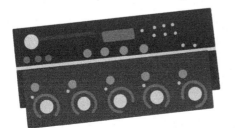

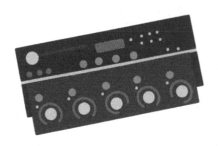

10

Kaila Mullady: Beatboxing Brilliance

Twenty-year-old Kaila Mullady arrived for her first-ever beatboxing competition feeling positive. Outside, groups of men warmed up in "ciphers"—small circles of people where beatboxers jam. Hearing them spit out rapid-fire sounds at impossible speeds, Kaila felt her confidence depart.

Was this a big mistake? What if she opened her mouth and nothing came out . . . again?

The best 16 beatboxers in the United States were competing, and she was the only female. If she didn't do well, it would reflect poorly on other women and girls trying to break into the male-dominated world of beatboxing.

She wanted to run. Instead, Kaila Mullady took the stage.

White-hot lights beat down on her. The room was small, the speakers thunderous. She would hear every beat, every mistake she made, and so would the judges.

Kaila was afraid, but she had faced greater fears performing on street corners in New York City. She would face this fear too.

Still, as she approached her very first battle, Kaila prayed to be pitted against someone easy.

Her opponent took the stage. He was the reigning champion. So much for easy.

In beatbox battles, there are two rounds. The contenders alternate, each performing for 90 seconds per round. The champ beatboxed, Kaila beatboxed, champ again, Kaila again.

Then the judges deliberated. Time slowed down for Kaila.

Since entering the world of beatboxing, she had heard over and over again, "It's impossible for girls to do low notes and it's impossible for girls to go fast." When a guy lost at beatboxing, no one said, "All guys are terrible beatboxers." But when a girl lost, it was all-too-often interpreted as proof of female inferiority.

Well-meaning friends had prepared her to accept failure. From the outset, they'd reminded her that only one girl had ever gotten into the national championship competition, so she shouldn't feel bad if she didn't make it. Then, when Kaila *had* gotten in, they'd predicted she would never beat a guy head-to-head.

Kaila stood on the stage waiting what felt like 40 years for the judges to declare the winner.

Now, they were pointing at her.

Kaila Mullady had just become the first girl ever to beat a guy in a national competition—first in the United States and first globally.

This was incredible. Now surely everyone would stop saying that girls couldn't beatbox.

Giddy at what she'd achieved, Kaila approached her opponent to give him a high five. Instead, he pulled her in really close and said, "You only won because you are a girl."

Kaila grew up in Long Island, New York, surrounded by her large Irish American family. She loved music from infancy, and by the time she was a toddler, she was making it *her* way. She would assemble her mother's pots and pans on the kitchen floor and drum until someone made her stop. She'd also empty the family's Kleenex boxes—scattering tissues everywhere—and turn them into rubber band guitars. That got her sent to her room.

No problem. Stripped of instruments, Kaila made music with her mouth. But she didn't just sing, she made all kinds of sounds—drums, vocal scratches, mouth trumpet, lip buzzing, click rolls. She couldn't name those sounds back then; she just knew she loved making them.

It wasn't until fifth grade that a kid told her, "You're beatboxing." Wow! There was a name for what she did.

Beatboxing became a favorite party trick. Kaila would beatbox in the lunchroom or on the school bus, and other kids would rap to her beats.

Beatboxing Basics

The first sounds beatboxers learn to make are the drums and hi-hat cymbals: P + T + K, each coupled with a strong puff of air. "P" mimics the kickdrum. "K" is the snare. "T" is the hi-hat sound.

Beatboxers like Kaila can make up to four different sounds at the same time, sometimes incorporating hand techniques. They can sing and do percussion simultaneously, a beatboxing technique called "epenthesis," where percussive sounds are placed in the middle of words.

Some of Kaila's favorite beatboxing sounds are pips, clickrolls, liprolls, trumpets, throat bass, and scratches. Learn Beatboxing 101 from Kaila on her YouTube channel.

When Kaila was 12 (2005), YouTube hit the Internet, and she knew just what to search for: beatboxing. The people in those videos—mostly guys—were uber-talented. To Kaila, they seemed like aliens, and reaching their level looked impossible. Beatboxing wasn't like piano where you could sign up for lessons, so she figured she'd better stick to her party tricks.

One musical goal that did look attainable though was singing with her middle school's show choir. Kaila practiced singing "Colors of the Wind" for three days prior to tryouts. She sang it for everyone—her mom, her grandma, her dog, even her dolls.

By audition day, she was ready. But when she heard the first note, she froze. She was shaking and sweating.

When she opened her mouth to sing, nothing came out.

Then Kaila heard what sounded like "an old bicycle horn, squeaking and honking." It was coming from her throat.

Sure, she made honking sounds when she beatboxed, but she was supposed to be singing. It was awful.

Kaila vowed never to sing publicly again.

For years, she honored that vow. As a senior in high school, she was in the school chorus, but everyone, even the director, knew she was lip synching.

Kaila still felt comfortable beatboxing for an audience though. Little did she realize when she made trumpet sounds with her voice that she was, in fact, singing.

Kaila was also interested in theater, and she began taking improv classes during high school. It was the perfect emotional outlet.

Her parents were divorcing, and there was a lot of tension in her home. But Kaila didn't think she could share her feelings outright. Instead, she wrote monologues for drama class and pretended she'd found them in obscure plays. Performing those monologues allowed her to express her bottled-up emotions.

In 2012, Kaila jumped off a cliff—well, off a sand dune to be exact. It wasn't the best idea. She was hanging out in the dunes with friends, and when she jumped, she expected a short fall, a soft landing, and "a fun slide down a sandy slope." Instead, she jumped too far out, dropped a long distance, and landed on flat, hard-packed sand, breaking her back.

Recovery would take close to a year.

After graduating high school, Kaila had begun performing with an improv group, but how could she possibly do physical comedy wearing a back brace? Unless a scene required a coat rack, a robot, or a tree, improv was out.

She lay in bed for two weeks wondering how to turn this negative situation into a positive one. During that time Kaila watched the 2012 Beatbox Battle World Championship (BBBWC) streaming from Berlin. Beatboxing was so new that this was only the third world championship ever held.

Unlike US competitions, the BBBWC separated the men and women. At first, Kaila scoffed. Why did other countries segregate beatboxers by gender as if it were a physical sport? Exceptional musicianship had nothing to do with gender.

Then again, these women were showing their stuff on a world stage.

Butterscotch Takes the Stage

Crowned the first female Beatbox Battle World Champion in 2005, Butterscotch (Antoinette Clinton) earned the respect of the mostly male American beatboxing community and paved the way for Kaila's success.

In 2007, Butterscotch placed third on *America's Got Talent*. Today, she performs worldwide singing, beatboxing, and accompanying herself on guitar and piano. Her original songs blend hip-hop, soul, jazz, and reggae and speak courageously and candidly about her life as "a biracial queer woman of color," her struggles with depression, and her stand for acceptance and inclusion.

A passionate advocate for prison reform, Butterscotch has performed for inmates at San Quentin State Prison in California. Her mission is "to empower and elevate people through music and compassion."

Now, while watching Pe4enkata (Adriana Nikolova) of Bulgaria win the 2012 BBBWC female championship, Kaila formulated a plan. The next world championship would be held in three years, and Kaila was going to enter it and win. This was how she would turn her broken back into a positive. After all, she could still beatbox in a back brace.

Just prior to her accident, Kaila had finally connected with the New York beatboxing community. A well-respected beatboxer named JFlo had heard her beatbox at a party and invited her to hang out with him.

Kaila had always assumed there were just "a few random people that beatboxed online." Then JFlo introduced her to his friends, a local community of beatboxers dedicated to pushing the art form forward. They were generous, creative people who loved to invent new sounds and share them with others. Kaila had found her teachers.

When her new friends beatboxed, Kaila was close enough to really hear the sounds and identify how they were made, which skyrocketed her skill level. She was now making sounds she'd once considered out of reach.

Then JFlo introduced her to Kid Lucky, a mentor who would push Kaila beyond her perceived limits and help her master her craft. Kid did beat rhyming—a combination of talking, rapping, or singing and beatboxing—and he was one of the best. He insisted Kaila beat rhyme too. And that meant singing.

Kaila had not sung lyrics in front of anyone since that dreadful day in sixth grade. But Kid Lucky was adamant. She would beat rhyme in public or she could find another mentor.

Kaila wanted to study with Kid so she agreed to jump off another cliff, a metaphorical one this time. She would do the thing she feared the most. She would sing on New York City street corners in front of thousands of people.

Every day Kid put Kaila on a corner with her amp and microphone, insisting she add words to her vocal percussion. And despite being terrified every single time, Kaila sang.

She still lived on Long Island, about two hours by train from New York City. Every day her goal was to make enough money to pay the round-trip train fare to and from the East Village. On a good day, earning the fare took two hours; on a bad day, it took five or six. Some days she drew a crowd and made a hundred dollars. On others, she only made two dollars.

To Kaila's surprise, people liked her singing voice. Club managers who stopped to listen invited her to perform in shows and at open mic nights.

By the time her broken back healed, the emotional wound associated with singing publicly had also healed. Kaila decided not to return to her improv group. Beatboxing was now her profession.

In 2013, she entered a video of herself beatboxing for an American beatboxing competition, made it into the top 16, walked out on the national stage, won her first beatbox battle, and became the first girl to ever beat a guy in a national competition. Then her opponent said those devastating words: "You only won because you are a girl."

But how had Kaila actually won that battle? She wasn't as fast or as loud as the guy she'd beat. She had something else going for her. Thousands of hours of beatboxing and beat rhyming coupled with her improv experience had produced a storyteller. When Kaila performed, she took her audience on a journey. Every performance was electrifying because Kaila's audience couldn't predict where she would take them next.

She lost her second battle in that competition, but she savored her victory nonetheless, committed to blazing a trail for the girls coming up behind her.

Then, three years after watching the livestream with a broken back, Kaila won the 2015 BBB World Championship Individual Female division, just as she planned. She won again in 2018, making her the only two-time world champion female beatboxer to date.

In the annual unsegregated American Beatbox Championships, Kaila won more and more battles against men. She was named 2014 American Beatbox Vice Champion. She was also a three-time American Beat Rhyming Champion and three-time American Loop Station Champion.

Kaila and her partner, Mark Martin, also compete in beatbox tag team battles under the name Power Couple and perform as the musical duo Lightship.

What Is a Loop Station?

A loop station is a portable recording device operated with a foot pedal so a musician can record a section of music then play it back "on loop" so it repeats. Beatboxers use a loop station to build layers of vocal percussion, sound effects, and harmonies to create a unique musical experience. Loop station beatbox competitors do this in front of a live audience. A multi-instrumentalist, Kaila has recorded a number of loop station YouTube videos where she layers in vocal harmonies, vocal percussion, and even guitar. Check them out!

Today, Kaila limits her battles to international competitions only. She no longer competes in the American Beatbox Championships and Mexican Beatbox Championships—the most significant platforms for beatboxers in North America—because she now produces them! Of course, under Kaila's leadership, those national championships continue to pit women against men.

She remembers when there were only about four professional women beatboxers in all New York City. Two of those women, Butterscotch and MC Beats (Meghan Costa), opened doors for Kaila. Now Kaila is uplifting the new generation of musicians practicing the artform.

Kaila says her purpose in life is "helping kids find the power of their voice and express themselves authentically." She teaches beatboxing to groups and individuals and travels the world inspiring elementary, high school, and college students with her story.

In a world where most people still consider what she does a party trick, Kaila is breaking down other barriers. She and Mark created a speech therapy curriculum that utilizes beatboxing. Their approach was inspired by Kaila's cousin, who was bored and unmotivated by his speech therapy sessions until Kaila turned the exercises into beatboxing practice.

The experimental curriculum led Kaila and Mark to a partnership with New York University. It also allowed them to teach beatboxing in a school for students who are visually impaired and have multiple disabilities—an opportunity Kaila found deeply rewarding.

It turns out that kids work harder to pronounce sounds and practice more on their own when the end result is beatboxing. Their curriculum is still being studied. Meanwhile, Kaila and Mark are teaching speech-language pathologists their techniques and have founded The Academy of Noise "to help people of all ages express themselves and find the power of their voice through beatboxing, writing, and storytelling."

In the midst of all this innovation, Kaila got a call from Shockwave, a beatboxer she sometimes substituted for on improv shows. This time he didn't need a sub.

"What are you doing this fall?" he asked. "Would you like to come to Broadway?"

Shockwave was in the cast of *Freestyle Love Supreme (FLS)*, a show produced by Lin-Manuel Miranda (*Hamilton* and *In the Heights*), and they needed another beatboxer with improv skills. A role on Broadway? Kaila was in!

On October 2, 2019, she opened in *FLS*, Broadway's first full-length musical improv show. It ran until January 2020, closing just before the pandemic shut down Broadway theaters. In fall 2021, *FLS* won a Special Tony Award, and Kaila and the cast returned to Broadway for a second run. In 2022, Kaila toured the United States with the show.

Kaila Mullady found her voice, and it led her to stages small and large—from street corners to school auditoriums, to world competitions, to Broadway and beyond.

She faithfully practices beatboxing every single day. And yes, the nerves are still there, even after two Broadway runs. So Kaila "practices being nervous."

Then she goes for it!

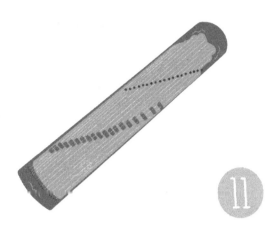

Vân-Ánh Vanessa Võ: Tradition and Improvisation

On December 4, 2021, San Francisco Bay Area music lovers crowded into Zellerbach Playhouse in Berkeley, donning masks and flashing vaccination cards, to witness a sold-out world premiere. In that performance of *Songs of Strength*, Vân-Ánh Vanessa Võ and her Blood Moon Orchestra offered traditional music's answer to contemporary questions. Among them, the 86,400 challenge.

The latter asks you to imagine that $86,400 is deposited in your bank account every morning. It's all yours. The only catch: you must spend it. You can't transfer it to savings, you can't invest it. Use it or lose it! If the idea sounds far-fetched, consider the fact that everyone wakes in the morning with that amount of a precious commodity, namely time—the 86,400 seconds in each day.

How should *you* spend it?

During the concert, the song "86,400" wrestled with the question in lines like these by colyricist Kev Choice:

> I walk the intersection
> Between struggles and blessings
> Learning life's lessons
> You will be uplifted if you listen to the message
> Every second, is destined
> No time like the present

It's hard to imagine an artist better poised to explore themes of presence and intention than Vân-Ánh Võ. From a very early age, she dedicated her daily 86,400 to one thing—music. And for her, the future always lay in songs of the past.

The Võ family settled in the famed artists' quarter of Hanoi, Vietnam, in 1976, following Vân-Ánh's father's return from the war. Their government-assigned studio apartment was small (less than half the size of an average classroom), but it was perfectly placed. In this neighborhood, musicians lived chockablock, and many different genres mingled in the soundscape.

Every morning, young Vân-Ánh woke to the sound of music all around her. On one side, she could hear someone practicing Cải Lương (Southern Vietnamese folk opera); on the other, Western opera; to the front, traditional music; to the back, the new rhythms of American rock. At the time, Vân-Ánh didn't know what effect the sound would have on her. But it all went in "drop by drop," filling her creative well.

The Võ home was happy—a place of love, though not luxury. Beyond the joyful noise, remains of war were everywhere. The washbasin and garbage bins were made from artillery shells and the school bell was fashioned from parts of a downed B-52 bomber.

As the country rebuilt, people were drawn to new and Western things, including classical music, regarding them as "beautiful" and "high class." But six-year-old Vân-Ánh didn't see it that way.

When her parents suggested saving for a cello, she politely declined. Vân-Ánh simply didn't like the look of the enormous instrument. Ditto for the funny way it sat between an artist's knees. But when she spotted someone playing traditional music on the street, it was love at first sight. Vân-Ánh adored how the đàn tranh (Vietnamese zither) lay elegantly in the artist's lap, how the musician moved with it. "I thought, *that* is beautiful. . . . I'd like to learn that!"

And in another stroke of destiny, her father and first music teacher, the late Võ Tuấn Minh, found a đàn tranh for Vân-Ánh to call her own. The national theater, where he worked as a musician, was ready to throw out the retired instrument, deemed damaged beyond repair. But he suspected that it had a little more life in it, and he was right.

Đàn Tranh

The đàn tranh is a zither with a long wooden sound-box and steel strings strung across movable bridges. It belongs to a family of instruments that originated in China as the guzheng and spread through Southeast Asia, where it became the Japanese koto, the Korean gayageum, and the Mongolian yatga. Farther from home, it gave rise to India's sitar and the harp in the West.

Like children growing up and moving out, the instrument had to "adapt to the culture" of its host countries. In Vietnam, the thick silk strings of the Chinese instrument evolved into thinner metal strings with a softer sound and higher pitch. Those flexible strings allow players to develop novel pitch-bending techniques, producing music that reflects the highly tonal character of the Vietnamese language.

In traditional music, performers pluck up and down the pentatonic scale—*hò-xự-xang-xê-cống* or *do-re-fa-sol-la*—with the right hand (thumb, index, and middle fingers) and bend the strings with the left hand to create tonal ornaments.

Vân-Ánh's uncle, a carpenter, patched the cracks and holes in her first đàn tranh and even carved a flower into the area where the wood was most deeply damaged. But he couldn't disguise the sound—it was terrible. Vân-Ánh recalls with amusement, "Somehow I loved it."

For her, the problem wasn't noise—instead, the quiet of a missing music curriculum. Traditional music, also called "folk," comprises generations-old canons of songs that are passed down through family or community groups. Learning this kind of music required finding a master. But no one in the Võ family played the đàn tranh, and when Vân-Ánh began asking for lessons, no doors opened to her. Behind them, men were busy instructing their own relatives.

Fortunately, there was no rule barring Vân-Ánh from listening in. And when she discovered that a renowned master, the late Nguyễn Thế Thiệp, lived a mere bike ride away, she began peddling over after school. In time, Vân-Ánh found ways to make herself useful by, say, tidying the Nguyễn's house or running errands—anything to win the master's trust.

It took her three long years to earn a place as Master Nguyễn's apprentice, a role that more resembles that of adopted child than mere music student. But when, at last, Vân-Ánh could study with him, she picked up songs with remarkable speed, learning a new one every day.

Never mind the scarcity of opportunities for girls to perform. Never mind the abundance of negative attitudes about women in the performing arts. She followed her bliss. In doing so, she discovered a success strategy: "If you put yourself into something, you will be a successful person because that will help you to express yourself. Maybe nobody else can see it, but you see it."

In fact, others quickly took notice of Vân-Ánh. Her first master introduced her to others:

> One of my masters took me to spiritual cer-
> emonies. But as soon as I arrived, everyone
> rolled their eyes. You're not supposed to have a
> female player there. I just walked in and started
> to play. And as soon as I played, you could
> see people realize music is music and it didn't
> matter if you are male or female.

By the age of sixteen, Vân-Ánh's skill had grown and so had her ambition. She had her eye on the most prestigious event for any đàn tranh player: the national competition in Saigon.

Enrolling in the contest would allow her to travel for the first time ever.

Winning would earn her an enormous cash prize of $2,000.

More than money or adventure, though, Vân-Ánh longed for the gift given to the contest's top performer: a new instrument built by a famous maker in Saigon.

But she couldn't just stroll into the competition hall. A teacher must open the door by enrolling her, and her new master, Professor Ngô Bích Vượng of the Hanoi Conservatory of Music, wasn't prepared to take an unproven student and her cracked-flower instrument onto a national stage. And a master's word is final.

Master Musicians

Two masters, Nguyễn Hoà Bình and Ngô Bích Vượng, profoundly shaped Vân-Ánh's Western practice: "These two professors showed me the Western side of the music and how to work in an ensemble."

An early mentor, Nguyễn Hoà Bình trained Vân-Ánh for nearly a decade, from age eight. Now retired, she was a celebrated player who later served as director of the Hanoi College of Art.

Ngô Bích Vượng is a đàn tranh master, head of the Traditional Instrument Department at the Vietnam National Academy of Music (formerly the Hanoi Conservatory), and the recipient of numerous awards for her dedication to art and culture. In a kind of music that "can't be learned in one lifetime," Vân-Ánh still reaches out to Master Ngô, connecting with her "like a professor, a mother, a friend— you name it."

Instead of pursuing competition travel and a glamorous new đàn tranh, Vân-Ánh stayed home and scraped together cash for a used instrument, determined to be ready when the contest came around again.

She emptied her wallet—the equivalent of $10—for an old and odd đàn tranh in the back of a Hanoi music shop. The thing was missing bridges and tuning pins, and there was a hole in the instrument face. But the real issue was its size. It was almost one-third longer than a regular đàn tranh.

To this day, Vân-Ánh can't explain the design. However, her instinct that bigger might be better, providing a stronger sound and a more stable pitch, was correct.

Unfortunately, she wasn't the only one to spot this rare treasure. After the instrument was cleaned up and set aside, Professor Ngô strolled into the shop, spotted the refurbished đàn tranh, and wanted it. And a master's word is final.

But to everyone's surprise, Vân-Ánh walked away with the instrument.

Maybe it was the force of the young apprentice's character—her presence and intention.

Maybe the mouse residing in the đàn tranh had something to do with it.

In fact, an entire rodent family had taken up residence there! During refurbishment, the music shop owner discovered that the hole in the instrument face had been chewed by another determined female—a mother mouse. And inside the đàn tranh's hollow body was her nest of pink babies.

With the mice out, Vân-Ánh quickly moved in. Soon, that instrument became a home to her as well. And so began the best years of Vân-Ánh's young adulthood. "Happiness is something that you have to create for yourself," she says. "You have to find it . . . no one will give it to you." For Vân-Ánh, this meant making music, music, music with her 86,400 seconds each day.

She practiced until she'd learned the assigned conservatory pieces, and then—in secret—studied the songs reserved for older students. She practiced until she could tell—by small shifts in the position of bridges—whether someone else had handled her instrument between sessions. She practiced until she knew—by subtle changes in tension—when a string was near to breaking. Her 10-buck đàn tranh had become a "signature" instrument and a kind of extension of her body. With it, she could express anything. And she gave back to Hanoi's soundscape all the songs she'd heard in the Võ family studio as a child.

Vân-Ánh left home for the first time ever during the year of the contest. In Saigon, she and the two other competitors from the Hanoi Conservatory of Music shared everything—a single unfinished room in the home of a relative and a mattress on the floor, taxi fare and food, and a rigorous practice routine.

None of these things daunted Vân-Ánh. And despite a significant lack of home-turf advantage, she followed the advice that she now gives her own pupils—namely, be the very sharpest knife in the box. The one that "can do a lot of things," the one that "is not replaceable."

Vân-Ánh progressed through all three rounds of the contest—over a month of performing—to win the 1995 Vietnam National Championship Title and first prize for Best Presentation of Contemporary Music.

From that national stage, Vân-Ánh strolled onto the international music scene.

Doors were opening for the musician who, a decade earlier, had trouble getting a foot in. And since Vân-Ánh had learned to play other traditional instruments during her education—đàn bầu (monochord), đàn t'rung (bamboo xylophone), trống (traditional drums)—concert organizers could get multiple performers for the price of one by flying her out for a show. The travel took her farther and farther from Hanoi, farther from her beloved artists' quarter. Fresh out of college, she performed in more than two dozen different countries.

Vân-Ánh toured the United States as a musical ambassador, at a time when the US and Vietnam were reestablishing relations. And that's when she met Steven Huỳnh. A volunteer, Steven drove her to Bay Area gigs, which gave the two time to get to know each other. They stayed in touch over the next five years. In 2001, they married, and Vân-Ánh moved to California to raise a family.

Then—for the first time—the performing stopped. And her life grew unusually quiet.

In her new home, no Cải Lương—or any other type of Vietnamese music—streamed through the window with the morning sun. "No one actually knew about Vietnamese traditional music and culture in the right context," she recounts. "People knew about the Vietnam War—how bloody it was. But what about the culture?" Aside from funerals of friends, Vân-Ánh hardly set foot on a concert stage for the next ten years.

But during her decade of "hibernation," she didn't let precious seconds slip away.

Vân-Ánh recorded *Twelve Months, Four Seasons* (2002). She cocomposed *Daughter from Danang*, which was Oscar nominated and a Sundance Grand Jury Prize Best Documentary winner (2003), and *Bolinao 52*, an Emmy Award-winning film and soundtrack (2009). And in 2010, Vân-Ánh released a second album, *She's Not She*, recorded with award-winning composer Đỗ Bảo.

Though still unready for the stage, Vân-Ánh listened to the stories that other artists were telling in their shows. Her traditional training had taught her to *hear* as well as play music. And from her seat in the audience, she began to connect her personal narrative to others.

One strange day, a jazz musician invited Vân-Ánh to bring an instrument along to his concert to jam after the performance. At the time, the only "jam" she knew was traffic on congested San Francisco streets. But she discovered that she'd been training to improvise all her life.

Her traditional education was just as much about self-expression as it was adherence to a music canon and techniques. Once Vân-Ánh could reproduce a master's rendition of a traditional song, she was free to "fit herself" into it.

Jazz improvisation required innovation, however. To play the rapid key changes of that genre, Vân-Ánh had to redesign her đàn tranh. The way she sees it, her roots will always be in Vietnam, but like a sturdy tree, she must "breathe in" her surroundings to grow and bear fruit.

And Vân-Ánh started sharing that fruit far and wide—as master and artistic director of the Su Viet Ensemble in San Francisco, artist-in-residence in ethnomusicology departments at universities across the nation, and as a mentor to underserved youth in Vietnam and the San Francisco Bay Area.

At the suggestion of a friend, Vân-Ánh did an Internet search of concert venues, and she made a little list of places to share Vietnamese traditional music with a large audience. The result: in two short years, she had performed at Lincoln Center, the Kennedy Center, Carnegie Hall, and the London Olympic Games 2012 Music Festival (the latter with the Kronos Quartet).

Back in the studio, Vân-Ánh recorded a third album, *Three Mountain Pass*, with the Kronos Quartet as guest contributors on "Green River Delta." The album's title track was inspired by a poem by the eighteenth-century feminist Ho Xuan Huong, and the opening song, "Vọng Cổ," is an homage to her beloved Master Nguyễn. NPR picked *Three-Mountain Pass* for its Top 10 Best World Music Compilation of 2013.

An ambitious, emerging composer, Vân-Ánh wrote 30-plus commissioned pieces over the next five years, including "The Odyssey—From Vietnam to America" (2016), which explores the journeys of the Vietnamese people escaping war; "Tender" (2018), a work for aerial dance about the unlikely activists who fought for San Francisco's Tenderloin District; and "Polestar" (2019), a project for the Alonzo King LINES Ballet centered around the orienting North Star.

Through the darkness of 2020, Vân-Ánh shined light on the Bay Area's diverse talent. Reaching across genres, she collaborated with artists whose work once seemed the farthest thing from traditional Vietnamese music, but now didn't. Those artists included Kev Choice (rap), Joel Davel (marimba lumina), Kai Eckhardt (electric bass), Tunjie (breakdance), Jimi Nakagawa (taiko), and Mahsa Vahdat (vocals). Together, they created *Songs of Strength*, whose track "86,400" wraps up with these lines:

> Put it all in perspective
> It's all about relationships we all connected
> I walk the intersection
> Between struggles and blessings

If you look at Vân-Ánh Vanessa Võ now, you'll see a pioneer blazing a trail for traditional music-making in the modern world. She was the first Vietnamese American to perform at the White House, an artist laureate under the Obama administration, and the founder of Blood Moon Orchestra. She's also a multi-instrumentalist who, during the December 2021 concert at the Zellerbach Playhouse, covered Jimi Hendrix's 1967 classic "Purple Haze" on a centuries-old instrument, the đàn bầu, using a kind of whammy bar made from buffalo horn to shift sound into sky-high registers.

But Vân-Ánh is no rebel. She knows how to bend without breaking with tradition.

Regina Carter:
Call and Response

In Genoa, Italy, in a temperature-controlled vault protected by armed guards, sits "The Cannon"—a violin with a dark, powerful tone. Crafted in 1743 for violin virtuoso Niccoló Paganini, who bequeathed it to the city upon his death, it is rarely touched. In December 2001, Regina Carter made history as the first jazz musician and first African American to play it.

When Regina arrived two days before the concert, not a single ticket had been sold. The mayor of Genoa, a huge jazz fan, was all for the concert, as was the city committee that oversees the violin, but some naysayers thought playing jazz on such a precious instrument would damage it. Regina appreciated their reverence for the instrument but not their biases.

"This is ignorant," she said at a press conference. "People who think like this have closed minds. The thought that one culture of music is somehow higher or better than another is to be prejudiced. You have to grow out of that. What do you think I'm going to do? You think I'm going to bash it on the floor?"

Every word she said aired, unedited, on TV and radio. And the Genoans listened. By concert time, Genoa's 2,000-seat opera house was sold out.

Meanwhile, Regina was led into a small room packed with city officials, armed guards, and reporters, to rehearse with The Cannon. The violin case remained closed while the room temperature was adjusted and the curtains drawn. Someone brought in a small table and spread a velvet cloth on it, then decided it was the wrong table and brought another. At last, the case was opened, The Cannon was tuned and handed to Regina.

Inspired by thoughts of her mother, Regina played her mom's favorite song, "Amazing Grace." The melody soothed her nerves and seemed to calm the room.

Then Regina got to work learning the instrument. The body of the Cannon was much bigger than the body of Regina's own instrument, and its strings were much longer. Therefore, the notes, especially after third position, were nowhere near where she expected them to be.

The following night, with armed guards in the wings and at every exit, Regina played Paganini's violin. "There were times I would go to play a note, and the note wouldn't speak. We call them woof tones," she recalls. "And I would think Paganini was standing there, jabbing me, joking, 'Ha ha! See? Not gonna let you.'"

New York Times music reviewer A. G. Basoli, who was at the concert, noted, "Even without amplification, her duet of Billie Holiday's 'Don't Explain' with the pianist Vana Gierig filled the sold-out auditorium, and a cadenza in which she quoted Arvo Pärt's 'Fratres' and a Bach Ciaccona allowed her to display her expressiveness and instrumental skills."

Regina received multiple standing ovations after that performance. But waiting guards immediately whisked away The Cannon, and she had to play the encore on her own violin. She chose Thelonious Monk's "Misterioso," a tribute to the mysterious Paganini.

"When I went to play it," she recalls, "[my violin] sounded like a mouse. It freaked me out because the sound was so small in comparison and so quiet."

Regina seems to be the only one who noticed, because "Misterioso" brought the Genoese crowd to their feet again.

In one sense, that triumph in Genoa was nothing new. Regina has been pushing the boundaries of musical performance and upending expectations since the age of two.

Regina grew up in Detroit, Michigan. Her mother, Grace, a schoolteacher, and her father, Dan, an auto worker, introduced her to many types of music. She especially loved Ella Fitzgerald, whose vocals felt "like being wrapped in a big hug."

Her two older brothers took piano lessons. One day, two-year-old Regina sat down at the keyboard and played a familiar tune for their music teacher.

"Who taught her that?" the teacher asked.

No one.

Regina seemed ready for lessons, so their teacher recommended Anna Love, who taught very young children. Anna tried to teach Regina to read music, but each week Regina would arrive at her lesson with a colorful new drawing (not her sheet music), place it on the piano's music shelf, and proceed to play. Regina was playing by ear, not reading music. Anna didn't want to force her student to read or quell her creativity, so she recommended they wait a bit.

When Regina was four, Anna called Grace and told her that the Community Music School in Detroit was offering violin lessons using the Suzuki Method. This method, which starts with playing by ear, would be perfect for Regina.

Each week there would be a private lesson plus a Saturday group lesson. Some Saturdays, Regina's teacher introduced a relay-style game. She'd play a made-up melody on her violin, then pass the lead from student to student. Regina and her classmates were improvising!

Regina studied violin throughout her childhood. She also studied dance. The Carter children often put on shows in their backyard. Normally shy and quiet, Regina came to life on the backyard stage—singing, dancing ballet and tap, and playing violin.

In ninth grade, Regina attended Cass Technical High School in Detroit, where she majored in music. As a freshman, she was still quiet and shy, but one day she went to school, and according to Grace, came home "someone else."

Grace's once-introverted child was now outgoing and completely obsessed with becoming a great violinist. "This thing just hit me," Regina recalls, "and all I could think about was practice, practice, practice, practice." But skipping school to practice landed her on academic probation.

Fortunately, Grace was not about to let Regina fail. She "went above and beyond as a mom," even creating a daily attendance report for her teachers to sign. As a result, Regina buckled down.

Still, high school was painful. She struggled to fit in the entire first year. Cass Tech had 4,000 students, and it seemed like everyone belonged to a group except her.

Then Regina found Brainstorm.

A Detroit-based funk/R&B band, Brainstorm invited her to tour with them playing violin. Regina pleaded with Grace to let her go. Her mother allowed her to tour Thursdays through Sundays, provided she kept her grades up. She had a group!

Thanks to Brainstorm, she also found a new look. Like many of her classmates, she'd been straightening her natural hair—a daily struggle. But two female Brainstorm bandmates wore their hair in beaded braids. Regina soon followed suit. Her confidence soared both on- and offstage, and fitting in at school got a lot easier.

At Cass Tech, Regina studied classical violin, but her best friend, Carla Cook, was a jazz singer. When Carla introduced her to albums by jazz violinists Jean-Luc Ponty, Noel Pointer, and Stéphane Grappelli, Regina was amazed.

What Is Jazz?

Regina Carter calls jazz "America's classical music." Jazz uses syncopated rhythms and has a forward momentum called "swing." What makes it distinct is improvisation, which Regina defines as "making up a tune on the spot with harmonies that are already existing underneath."

Improvisation takes great skill. A jazz group will play the standard melody to a tune one time, then instrumentalists and vocalists will take turns making up melodies, while others play rhythm and harmonies and respond musically. Jazz can also include call-and-response, which is when one instrument or vocalist improvises a melody and another either echoes back the call or improvises a fitting response. And while these are traditional structures, jazz takes other forms and can even be through-composed (composed with different music for each verse).

One night, Regina and Carla saw violinist Stéphane Grappelli perform live with his jazz trio. What struck Regina, besides the sound, was the smile on Stéphane's face. No one smiled playing European classical music. But here was Stéphane having fun.

Regina wanted that energy. She wanted that fun. She wanted that freedom.

When Regina announced her desire to play jazz, Grace was not happy. She wanted her daughter to play in an orchestra's string section—a job with benefits and security. But Regina had always envisioned herself as a soloist, and jazz was the perfect pathway to soloing.

Regina continued playing European classical music, but she also found a home in Cass Tech's jazz band. Her classical violinist friends were supportive of her jazz obsession; her classical teachers were not.

Regina's string quartet got to play for Yehudi Menuhin, one of the greatest classical violinists of the twentieth century. This was a very big deal, and Regina played her best.

After the performance, one of her high school teachers told Yehudi, "She wants to play jazz. She's going to ruin her career."

Yehudi picked up his violin, played a little blues lick, and said, "Leave her alone."

After graduation, she entered the New England Conservatory in Boston, Massachusetts, to study classical music. After two miserable years there, she transferred to Oakland University (OU) in Rochester, Michigan, to study jazz.

OU's big band director knew exactly what to do with Regina. He seated her in the alto saxophone section. "Breathe when [the sax players] breathe, phrase how they phrase," he told her. "And stop listening to violin players. There's too few of you out there, and you're going to sound like them. You want to find your own voice."

Regina played the alto sax parts on her violin. At last, she was swinging.

Regina also played in Detroit jazz clubs with extraordinary musicians from all over. No matter how shy she felt, she always introduced herself and requested contact information. She was building her community.

After college, she taught strings in Detroit public schools for two years, taught violin on a US military base in Germany for two more, and finally settled in New York City. There, she contacted the New York musicians she'd met in Detroit to let them know she was living in the city and available for gigs.

Regina played everything: R&B with Aretha Franklin, rock with Billy Joel, country with both Dolly Parton and Tanya Tucker, hip-hop on the studio albums of Lauryn Hill and Mary J. Blige, and jazz with Straight Ahead, an all-female quintet. But when somebody told her, "Be careful doing all this different music . . . people are going to say you're not serious," Regina disagreed.

She recorded six albums with jazz ensembles and was soon leading and recording with her own quintet. Their first two albums, *Regina Carter* (1995) and *Something for Grace* (1997), got her noticed.

Regina was invited to tour with composer and trumpet player Wynton Marsalis and the Jazz at Lincoln Center Orchestra performing Wynton's *Blood on the Fields*—a jazz oratorio on slavery and freedom. During that tour, she wowed jazz fans and critics alike with her violin solos.

Her third album, *Rhythms of the Heart* (1999), further solidified her reputation. For *Rhythms*, Regina insisted on recording a wide range of styles—Afro-Cuban, bossa nova, blues, swing, R&B, hard bop, and bebop. The resulting sound was pure Regina. She'd found her voice.

Other albums followed, including *Freefall* (2001), an album of duets with pianist Kenny Barron, which earned the duo a Grammy nomination.

Then, in 2004, Regina got married.

> My mother would always say to me, "Don't marry a jazz musician or your children will starve." What did I do? I married my drummer, Alvester Garnett. Alvester called my mom and asked for permission to marry me to which she said, "You know, she has her ways," then "Y'all are grown. I guess you know what you're doing, go ahead." Grace knew that Alvester was a good man and came from a good family or else her answer would have been a simple "humph." Alvester is incredibly smart, kind, and very supportive and makes me laugh every single day. I'm blessed.

That same year Regina's mother was diagnosed with cancer for the third time. When it became apparent that Grace was going to die, Regina stopped touring. For three months she spent every day at her mother's side. During those last days with Grace, Regina began to hear a new calling: to be of service to people who were dying.

Assured by Carla Cook, who told her, "God doesn't give us just one calling," Regina became a hospice volunteer. Sometimes she sits quietly and holds a dying person's hand, sometimes she plays her violin. Always, Regina listens. She even started training as a professional "death doula"—someone who supports people and families through the end-of-life.

Following her mother's death, Regina was awarded a MacArthur Fellows Program grant of $500,000. It couldn't have come at a better time. MacArthur "genius grants" are not awarded for past accomplishments. Rather, they are "an investment in a person's originality, insight, and potential."

The money allowed Regina to explore her African musical roots on her next album, *Reverse Thread* (2010). To find music, she listened to recordings of folk tunes from the African continent. Then she reimagined them. Watch the *Reverse Thread* NPR Music Tiny Desk concert. It's amazing.

Next, Regina turned to her American roots. To better understand her paternal grandfather, an Alabama coal miner whom she never knew, she listened to hundreds of old recordings—Cajun fiddle music, early gospel, and coal miners' work songs. She says, "The majority of the field recordings for *Southern Comfort* (2014) were single melody lines being sung by someone. So with each arranger, I asked them to maintain the beauty of these pieces, as naked as they were, but also to modernize them. Every arrangement is very unique and colorful, but the fact that they're all from the South is the thread that ties them together."

In 2017, she released *Ella: Accentuate the Positive*, to honor Ella Fitzgerald, the singer whose voice she loved as a child. Her friend Carla Cook sang on that album.

Nominating Kendrick Lamar

Regina has been named to the Pulitzer Prize for Music jury three times (2016, 2018, and 2020). The five-person jury works together to select three finalists from hundreds of entries. The 2018 jury, which Regina chaired, named Kendrick Lamar's "brilliant" hip-hop/pop album *DAMN.* as a finalist. Prior to 2018, Pulitzers had only been awarded for classical or jazz compositions, so everyone, including Regina, was surprised when the committee awarded the Pulitzer to Kendrick. Regina took the ensuing heat from fellow musicians in stride; she believes the Pulitzer's value is enhanced by including all music.

In 2018, Regina won the Doris Duke Artist Award: $250,000 to spend as she wished. So, of course, she went in a new direction, making an album that "strives to illuminate the power of democracy and serve as a beacon of hope." *Swing States: Harmony in the Battleground* (2020) contains tunes associated with all the US electoral swing states, and, yes, it swings.

The award is also helping fund Regina's multimedia project, *Gone in a Phrase of Air*, which spotlights the many vibrant communities across the United States that were systematically demolished in the name of urban renewal in the 1950s and 1960s, displacing hundreds of thousands of disadvantaged people of color and Indigenous Americans. *Gone in a Phrase of Air* both mourns and celebrates these lost places, including Black Bottom, the Detroit community where Regina's mother, Grace, grew up.

Like her mother, Regina is an educator at heart, and she takes every opportunity to develop educational projects and to mentor aspiring musicians. She serves as artistic director for the Geri Allen Jazz Camp (GAJC), a summer residency for female and nonbinary jazz performers ages 14 to 26 (see the resources section).

Regina believes the relationships students build at GAJC are as valuable as the skills they build. "This is your community," she tells them, "and some of you all are going to have these connections for the rest of your lives." She should know. Among the faculty at GAJC are some of Regina's lifelong friends, including jazz singer Carla Cook and bassist Marion Hayden.

Regina also teaches at the Manhattan School of Music in New York City. One of her classes is an improvisation elective for classical string players.

She starts the first day of class with a call-and-response game—a kind of musical conversation. Regina plays the violin and sings out questions to her students. They have to answer her back by singing their responses while playing what they sing on their instruments. Some of these musicians have never sung while playing. It's scary, but they go for it. Soon everyone is laughing.

Laughter. That's how Regina moves them through the fear. In her 2021 Commencement address at the UCLA Herb Alpert School of Music, she said:

> Music teaches us one of the most powerful lessons: that nothing is 100 percent certain. Music isn't stagnant, it's fluid. And its beauty comes from its imperfections. . . . You might think you're lost. But remember, you can discover some incredible things when you get lost.

In Regina's case, embracing the beauty and imperfections of a 260-year-old violin won her the respect of the Genoese people, who later invited her to return and record an entire album on Paganini's Cannon. Of course, being Regina, she ventured into unfamiliar musical territory and emerged with a moving masterpiece that marries classical, jazz, and film music. That album is aptly titled *Paganini: After a Dream*.

What will Regina dream up next?

Part V
Power to Produce

13

Nova Wav:
Songwriting and Producing Duo

Producing and songwriting duo Brittany "Chi" Coney and Denisia "Blu June" Andrews were riding to the Atlanta airport when their first song, "Tipsy Love," played on the radio. Recorded by talented Atlanta R&B singer Bobby V and rapper Future, the song was sure to be a hit. As their music pulsed through the vehicle, Chi and Blu June paused to savor the career-defining moment.

Then the song ended, and a popular Atlanta radio DJ proceeded to skewer it. He hated their song.

So, this was actually *not* the moment.

They rode in stunned silence.

But by the time they boarded their flight, the two were focused on the future. They had to be. They were flying to L.A. to write songs for possible placement on Rihanna's upcoming album.

Chi and Blu June landed in L.A. strong in their belief in themselves and in each other. They knew they were destined to succeed. Where did they get such unshakeable faith?

Chi was born in 1986, while her mother, Felicia, was in her sophomore year at the University of Florida (UF) in Gainesville. Thanks to Chi's two grandmothers, who both cared for Chi, her mother completed her elementary education degree uninterrupted.

After Felisha's graduation from UF in 1989, the mother and daughter moved to the family farm in Plant City, Florida. There Chi helped her grandfather tend the vegetables he grew for local grocers.

As for music, Chi recalls making up her own tunes on her grandparents' organ when she was only two or three. She later sang in the children's choir and did liturgical dance at church. She also played saxophone from fourth through tenth grade.

But Chi's obsession for most of her childhood was sports—especially gymnastics and basketball—where she shined.

Chi also excelled in math and science, attending Lincoln Academy, the STEM-focused magnet school in Lakeland, Florida, where her mother taught. Then, in her last year of middle school, Chi, her mother, and her father, Reginald, moved to Lawrenceville, Georgia, a suburb of Atlanta. There, the math, science, and art of music production finally got her attention.

"Music really found me again in high school," she says. One day she heard a guy in the hallway talking about making his own beats (instrumental tracks) on Fruity Loops, a digital audio workstation. Chi downloaded the software and started making beats and writing songs. She had a new obsession.

The stars magically aligned for Chi in twelfth grade though when her high school offered a music technology class. She took the class and officially became a music tech nerd.

Blu June grew up in Tallahassee, Florida, a middle child with an older sister and younger brother. Her dad, Ira, worked for the Department of Transportation, and her mom, May, worked for the Department of Corrections. Her grandfather was a minister, and the whole family sang in church. "It's a gift we all have," says Blu June.

Outside church, Blu June sang along to records by Lauryn Hill, Missy Elliott, and Anita Baker. She took piano lessons for a time but quit to focus on her other passion: sports.

Blu June was a stellar basketball player. During her freshman year, the coach encouraged her to attend varsity tryouts, but she hesitated. The other girls trying out were "so good."

Her dad had zero doubts though. He told Blu June she would make varsity—giving her the confidence to lace up her sneakers and go for it.

That was one of the last conversations Blu June ever had with her father. He passed away two weeks before her fifteenth birthday—before she knew she'd made varsity. He was her rock, and she turns to his memory for guidance still.

During high school, Blu June considered a career in music but chose to pursue a degree in sports management instead, attending the University of North Florida in Jacksonville on a basketball scholarship. After college, Blu June didn't find a good fit with a sports franchise, so she got a job in medical billing and set her sights on music—singing, rapping, and songwriting after hours.

A marketing major, Chi attended Savannah State University in Georgia, a historically black university, for two years, then transferred to Georgia State in Atlanta. The transfer was a good move.

In Atlanta, Chi heard about an internship opportunity at Grand Hustle Studios. They wanted students with an audio engineering background, which Chi didn't have.

"I'm just going to wing it," she told herself, "and I'll learn on the spot."

On the way to the interview, she studied a list of likely questions. Sure enough, the Grand Hustle interviewer asked five of them, and Chi gave the "right" answers, even claiming skills she didn't really have.

Could she use Pro Tools? Sure!

Chi got the internship, then she learned Pro Tools—fast!

The internship taught her to "embrace the hustle of it." Chi started at the studio's front desk as receptionist, but she didn't mind. Having the opportunity to greet T. I. (the studio's famous owner) and industry icons like Timbaland and Justin Timberlake "was dope!" And eventually, Chi graduated to postsession cleanup and even learned engineering basics.

At Grand Hustle, Chi was surrounded by men, but she found a female role model in the studio's business manager, Hannah Kang. Chi says, "I picked up some of her surety and confidence. She didn't bow down to men. She told them what to do and they listened."

While in college, Chi also became obsessed with another role model, Beyoncé. She watched *The Beyoncé Experience* DVD every single day for a year.

Back in Tallahassee, Blu June was working "what seemed like full time" on music after putting in long days doing medical billing. She hated the spotlight that came with being an artist but was willing to put up with it to do the part she loved—writing songs.

Then one day someone in the industry suggested, "You should just be a songwriter."

What? Blu June had just assumed artists wrote their own songs. The knowledge that many artists rely on songwriters changed everything.

"I started concentrating on writing songs and learning more about the songwriting process," she recalls. Blu June studied the work of her hero, Ester Dean, and wrote tracks for local artists. She was writing solo, but that would soon change.

The Song Factory: Ester Dean

"Ester Dean did a lot for music in a very short amount of time," says Blu June. Singer, songwriter, and actor Ester

Dean has written and produced R&B, hip-hop, pop, and dance music hits for artists from Beyoncé to Usher. Her first number-one single was Rihanna's "Rude Boy" and her second was Katy Perry's "Firework." No wonder they call her "The Song Factory."

Around 2009, a rapper from Tallahassee hit Chi up on Facebook: "I ran across your old MySpace page. Can you send me a couple of tracks?"

Chi e-mailed him a song she'd been working on.

He responded, "I love the tracks. I'm gonna have this girl I met come over and do the hook." A hook is a memorable musical and/or lyrical phrase that pulls listeners in. It is usually danceable and recurs multiple times.

When Chi heard the hook, she thought, "Oh, my God, who is that girl? Her voice is amazing!"

It was Blu June.

The duo began collaborating remotely.

"Chi was sending tracks through e-mail," says Blu June, "and I would record myself via Garageband."

Garageband? Chi insisted Blu June learn Pro Tools, the industry standard.

They swapped tracks and texts for four months before they finally spoke.

A year in, they met in person. The chemistry was real, and Chi convinced Blu June to move into her parents' house in Atlanta.

The duo called themselves Nova Wav. A nova is a huge nuclear explosion in a binary star system whose orbits grow so close that material from one star's surface is pulled onto the other, making the light emanating from a nova up to 100,000 times brighter than normal. A wav is a type of electronic music file. The metaphor fit this duo perfectly.

Naming themselves individually was another powerful step. Each chose her name with great care and an eye toward the future they're creating together.

Denisia Andrews named herself "Blu June" after her dad, Ira Andrews Jr., whose fraternity brothers called him "Blu" and whose family called him "June." "I carry him with me everywhere I go," she says.

Brittany Coney named herself "Chi" after studying the word's multiple meanings: (1) In Igboland (the indigenous homeland of the Igbo people in Southeastern Nigeria), Chi means "source being" or "Creator." When someone calls Chi's name, she feels that God is with her, protecting her, and guiding her response. (2) Chi or Qi refers to a form of healing energy (see chapter 6), and according to Chi's mom, her daughter has "healing hands." (3) Chi Rho is the Greek symbol for "Christos," Jesus Christ. Yes, it's a powerful name.

In 2012, Blu June and Chi, now more than two years into their partnership as Nova Wav, found themselves in that Uber listening in stunned silence as the DJ lambasted their first record. The duo had no time to be devastated though. They got out of that car, boarded their L.A.-bound flight, and visualized success at the Rihanna camp.

It turns out that focusing on faith and the future they envision is Nova Wav's superpower.

What Is a Camp?

A camp is a kind of creative collective where an artist's executive producer brings in a bunch of songwriters and audio producers and divides them into small groups, in which they write songs.

At the camp, Blu June and Chi were given a track to which Future had written the hook. They were asked to write the verses. "It's like you get thrown in the pool," says Blu June, "and then what you gonna do? Are you gonna sink or swim?"

They swam. Two weeks later, they'd locked in a placement on Rihanna's *Unapologetic* album with "Loveeeeeee Song," which would become one of the Grammy-winning album's biggest hits.

So they had a hit, then . . . nothing.

For the next two years, they kept writing, improved their production skills, and built relationships with artists. Finally, they got another song placement, "Big Mistake," the promotional single for Ariana Grande's album *My Everything* (2014), which would go triple-platinum.

Recording Industry Association of America Certification

The Recording Industry Association of America certifies records based on the number of units sold:

- Gold album: 500,000 units
- Platinum album: 1 million units
- Multiplatinum album: 2-plus million units
- Diamond album: 10 million units

A "unit" is:

- One digital or physical album sold/shipped, or
- 10 tracks from the album downloaded, or
- 1,500 audio or video streams of songs from the album

One ingredient they wish they'd had early on was a female mentor they could have turned to for advice in the male-dominated world of producing. However, the lack of support made the duo extremely self-sufficient. Between them, they can perform every role in a recording session.

Blu June and Chi commuted between Atlanta and L.A. for four years. Then, on the way home from a Mary J. Blige camp in 2013, they had a realization: "Nothing ever happens for us until we're in L.A." So they moved to Hollywood "just to see what would happen."

Their new Hollywood apartment included a vision board with images of Beyoncé and Jay-Z. Six days after they moved in, they got a call. Someone had canceled on Hit-Boy, who was working on Beyoncé and Jay-Z's first joint studio album. Could they fill in?

"They put us in a private room, and we wrote a song," Chi recalls. "Then they came knocking three or four hours later, and they were like 'Yo, Jay-Z's in here. He listened to your song and wants to meet you guys.' . . . So we walked into the room, and Jay-Z was going crazy over the song. We watched him record it that night. He was freestyling off the top of his head. It was really insane."

They created and recorded a bunch of songs with Jay-Z and Beyoncé over the ensuing weeks, and although none of those songs made it on to the album, they now had a working relationship with the couple.

Certain they were on the right path, Nova Wav kept the faith.

Both Chi and Blu June are deeply spiritual. They begin every studio session with prayer, kicking everyone out of the room except their Creator, and putting it all in God's hands.

Working alone also allows them to make mistakes without fear. They are very comfortable with each other. Blu June usually takes the mic, where she hums melodies and tries out lyrics, while Chi works the console and produces, but they have no problem trading places. They trust each other's judgment. If one feels strongly about something, the other backs her.

According to Chi:

Blu June is extremely, extremely magical . . . just being able to pull things together, putting it in a pot and making it her own. She's amazing at melody and at taking something that's very complicated and making it plain English—but also very witty. She's got swagger: her mic presence, it's insane! She's a dope individual, just moving with God, moving with love.

And Blu June has this to say:

Chi's a leader. She's confident. She knows what she wants. And I'm so happy God paired me with somebody like that because in this industry we have to make a lot of decisions. And she doesn't second-guess herself. She's super intelligent. People turn to her and trust her. There's times when we've gone into a session just to write, not necessarily to produce, and people will be asking her what to do.

Nova Wav's motto is "Be braver sooner," words they first heard while watching a video of Teresa LaBarbera Whites, the executive producer who discovered and developed Beyoncé. "It just felt so holy," says Chi, "so we carry that with us everywhere."

When asked how their songwriting experience influences them as producers, Blu June says, "We make room for the voice. It's the most important instrument. We've learned to use the right instruments to complement certain vocal tones or certain melodic cadences."

Adds Chi, "When it comes to a song, the lyrics and the melody are the most important parts. So, as a producer, you don't have to be so busy doing all of these extra musical things because the lyrics and melody are going to take care of it for you."

As the industry's only prominent Black female producing duo, they've dealt with their share of stereotyping. Others tried to relegate them to hip-hop and R&B music only, but they've made their mark with pop songs as well. And they've had to prove that hiring a female duo can provide artists with exponential producing power.

"We just have to be good," says Blu June, "because being good brings the people to you." And indeed, the people have come.

In 2018, they got the *ultimate* call. Could they jump on a flight to Wales and come work with Beyoncé and Jay-Z for a few days?

Of course they'd come!

The moment they had been visualizing for years was here. As they flew over the Atlantic Ocean, the two pictured a positive, productive meeting. They arrived confident, excited, unafraid.

"And when we got around them," says Chi, "it felt like home."

Of Beyoncé, Blu June says, "She's a genius, and she's intense. She's probably one of the most creative people we've ever worked with. And she demands excellence."

Nova Wav had no problem bringing excellence to the project the Carters were working on in Wales. It was *Everything Is Love*, the as-yet-unreleased album they'd worked on in L.A. four years earlier. This time, however, Nova Wav's songs made the cut. They cowrote and produced "LoveHappy" and cowrote on "Nice," "Friends," and "Black Effect" as well. *Everything Is Love* went on to win a Grammy for Best Urban Contemporary Album.

Blu June and Chi also worked with Beyonce on *The Lion King: The Gift*, an album on which they have four credits.

They know they are blessed and feel they have a duty to something bigger than themselves. On that matter, they quote Tupac Shakur, who said, "I will spark the brain that will change the world."

Nova Wav is out to spark change. Themes that recur throughout their work include love, self-respect, and women's empowerment. They never portray women as victims.

They cowrote on Beyoncé's critically acclaimed single "Black Parade," a song celebrating Black history and Black activism that dropped on Juneteenth in 2020 and garnered Beyoncé a Grammy for Best R&B Performance.

Remembering how hard it was for them coming up, the duo has taken on mentoring aspiring female producers through Alicia Keys's nonprofit, She Is the Music (see resources section), a process they find humbling and rewarding.

Equally humbling—and astonishing to them—is how big the Nova Wav brand has gotten. They've written and produced songs with Britney Spears, DJ Khaled, H.E.R., Jason DeRulo, Kehlani, Kelly Clarkson, Mary J. Blige, Monica, Nicki Minaj, Saweetie, Teyana Taylor, and more. They also signed a publishing deal with Warner Chappell Music, have two songs in the film *A Wrinkle in Time*, released a downloadable Nova Wav "Girls Do It Better" sample pack of their signature sounds on Splice, and wrote and produced a song for a Lexus commercial in which they also acted. (Catch it on YouTube.)

The duo was nominated for two 2022 Grammy Awards: Album of the Year for H.E.R.'s *Back of My Mind* (as producers and songwriters) and Best R&B Song for "Pick Up Your Feelings" from Jazmine Sullivan's *Heaux Tales* album (cowritten with Jazmine Sullivan and Kyle "Kxhris" Coleman). "Pick Up Your Feelings" won Jazmine a Best R&B Performance Grammy and *Heaux Tales* was awarded Best R&B Album.

As artists, they are always learning. Blu June keeps up with pop culture because staying current is critical to writing song lyrics that resonate with their audience. And Chi watches YouTube tutorials to continue developing her engineering, mixing, production, and songwriting skills. They encourage women they mentor to do the same, saying, "If nothing's happening in your career, you can always be at work honing your craft."

At this point, "nothing's happening" has ceased to be a concern for Nova Wav. The duo is truly a nova—a pair of bright stars lighting up the galaxy of music production and songwriting.

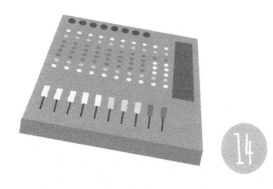

Maria Elisa Ayerbe: Engineering Latin Sound

Maria Elisa Ayerbe walked out on HBO Latino's stage and greeted her guest, renowned singer Carlos Rivera.

"Welcome to *A Tiny Audience*," she said. "It's a pleasure to have you here."

"On the contrary," said Carlos. "I am very happy, especially because I get to be with you, Maria Elisa."

Laughing, she replied, "Why? What did I do?"

"You do everything," Carlos said. "You are a person who opens doors, opens roads, so that many more women can also be represented in the industry."

Maria Elisa gracefully steered the conversation back to Carlos's career. But surely millions of HBO Latino television viewers were left wondering what doors she was opening for women in music.

It was 2021, and hosting a TV show centered on Latinx performers was just the latest twist in Maria Elisa Ayerbe's extraordinary career in music production and engineering—an occupation where only 2.6 percent of working professionals are women. The Grammy Award nominee, Latin Grammy winner, and multi–Latin Grammy nominee is also a university professor. She has her own independent record label. And in 2019 she was honored by the Latin Recording Academy with the Leading Ladies of Entertainment award for "outstanding performance as a professional and socially conscious woman within the arts and entertainment fields, inspiring the next generation of female leaders."

How did Maria Elisa become a leader in a field that barely existed in her home country when she was a teen? How did she even *find* the doors she is now opening for other women?

Maria Elisa was born in Bogotá, Colombia, in 1984. Her father, Guillermo Ayerbe, worked as an architect, and her mother, Clara Marcela Barona, was a social communicator who produced television shows, documentaries, and media campaigns for socially conscious organizations. She also has a younger brother, Nicolas Ayerbe Barona (now a filmmaker).

As a child, Maria Elisa enjoyed playing soccer and roller-skating with neighborhood friends. Bogotá was scary though. All over the city, narcos (drug traffickers) retaliated against their enemies with car bombings. They also kidnapped people and held them for ransom. You never knew when a bomb would explode or a child would be kidnapped, so she was tightly supervised.

When Maria Elisa was in first grade, her mother took a job as a communications officer for UNICEF Colombia, and Maria Elisa often tagged along. During one UNICEF music recording session, Maria Elisa got to watch the engineer work the mixing board. The equipment fascinated her. Little did she know she was seeing her future.

On weekends, Maria Elisa listened to the records her dad played in their apartment—American rock bands, British artists, Spanish rock, Cuban jazz, and pop hits by Cuban American singer-songwriter Gloria Estefan.

Gloria Estefan: "Queen of Latin Pop"

Gloria Estefan had her first worldwide hit shortly after Maria Elisa was born. By age four, Maria Elisa was a Gloria Estefan superfan. With more than 75 million records sold, Gloria is one of the all-time best-selling female singers. Her many honors include three Grammys, the Presidential Medal of Freedom, a Kennedy Center Honor, and induction into the Songwriters Hall of Fame.

Maria Elisa watched a lot of TV as a child, and she was a big fan of *MTV Unplugged*, a show where rock bands played acoustic versions of their songs. When she was nine, American grunge band Nirvana performed on *MTV Unplugged*. That iconic episode was released a year later as an album, *MTV Unplugged in New York*, and Maria Elisa was determined to learn to play it on guitar.

Her dad lent her an acoustic guitar that he had never used, and without instruction, Maria Elisa, age 10, trained herself to tune it by ear. Within six months, she'd taught herself to play every guitar lick from that Nirvana album.

At that point, her parents hired a guitar teacher. Maria Elisa worked hard between lessons, proving to her parents that she was serious. Then, when she begged her dad for an electric guitar, he bought the cheapest model he could find, which turned out to be an "amazing" Yamaha.

It didn't come with an amplifier though. Undaunted, 11-year-old Maria Elisa wired the guitar to a tinny stereo boombox for amplification. She played that way for months until her parents finally bought her a four-watt amp the size of a water bottle. Grateful, she used that tiny amp for years to come.

Maria Elisa had fun playing guitar and singing, but she also enjoyed public speaking. In high school, she excelled at speech, debate, and poetry readings and participated in Model UN, a program that educates students in diplomacy, international relations, and how the United Nations resolves issues.

Maria Elisa was also goalie and captain of her high school soccer team. During a tournament game in Bogotá, she dove for the ball and broke three small bones in her wrist. As a result, playing guitar was painful, so she stopped. That was okay. She had never envisioned a career in music anyway. She planned to go into international relations, law, or politics.

But changes were coming that would disrupt her plans. Her parents had career, security, and economic concerns. Colombia was experiencing a recession and was undergoing a violent guerilla and paramilitary insurgence. In addition, her mother wanted an international career. So, when a UNICEF post opened up in Bolivia, she took it. (She would later transfer to UNICEF Angola, where she was stationed for eight years.) Leaving friends was difficult for 16-year-old Maria Elisa. But the move to La Paz, Bolivia, brought welcome changes.

The Bogotá of Maria Elisa's youth was a crowded city of 8 million people, where everyone kept to themselves and rarely greeted one another. But the people in La Paz were warm, friendly, and welcoming. There, with bombings and kidnappings no longer a concern, Maria Elisa could also move about the city freely.

She made new friends, sang in the school choir, and took up a new instrument. Unlike her school in Bogotá, her new school had a band. She chose to play the clarinet because she could hold it comfortably with her injured wrist.

Maria Elisa finished high school and considered her future. She would attend university, but didn't know what to study. A degree in political science meant returning to Colombia to take a college entrance exam she wasn't prepared for.

Her mother had an idea. She said, "You know how you love music, and you are always trying to fix your Walkman? Well, there is a career that blends those two talents, it's called audio engineering!"

Maria Elisa loved working with electronic gear, had an ear for harmonies, rhythms, and musical arrangements, and was a natural leader. Audio engineering required all those talents. The more she learned about the field, the more excited she became. "I was totally down for that life," she says.

What Is Audio Engineering?

Audio engineers must know both the technical and artistic aspects of music production. The two primary jobs they perform are recording and mixing. The recording engineer selects, sets up, and operates the recording equipment and records songs.

Mixing happens either after a recording is made or in real-time during a live event. The mixing engineer mixes together multiple sounds, including lead and background vocals and all musical instruments. They manipulate each sound's volume, frequency, dynamics, and panoramic position to get just the right blend.

Maria Elisa soon found an audio engineering degree program at Universidad de Chile (UC) in Santiago. There was just one problem. When she told her calculus teacher, Sandra Reznicek, that she planned to be an audio engineer, Sandra laughed. "You're terrible at math. You're never going to make it."

Then, seeing how passionate and determined Maria Elisa was, Sandra added, "What are we going to do about it?" Together, they cooked up a plan. Maria Elisa would come to her classroom at lunchtime every day for tutoring. She would also take college prep classes in calculus and physics.

Their plan worked. Maria Elisa passed the UC entrance exam, including math and physics. She was in!

At UC, Maria Elisa aced music theory, and when she stepped into the university's recording studio, it was love at first sight. But despite working hard in algebra, calculus, physics, electronics, and acoustics, she often struggled with this "super advanced" STEM material.

Two and a half years in, Maria Elisa started looking for a program with less emphasis on math and physics, one centered on music. She found exactly that at Universidad Javeriana (UJ) in Bogotá. There she could pursue a five-year music degree with an emphasis in audio engineering. So, even though she only received credit for one of her UC classes, Maria Elisa transferred to UJ and started over.

While studying at UJ, she got her first professional gig assisting Colombian audio engineer José Pupo with a classical music recording session for the 90-piece Bogotá Philharmonic Orchestra. Every morning at 6:30, for 10 consecutive days, Maria Elisa and another assistant would set up 120 microphones. That might seem like busywork, but setting up the right types of microphones to capture so many different instruments takes knowledge and precision.

This was an opportunity to ingrain technical skills until she got them right. "Repeat, fail, repeat, fail, repeat, repeat, repeat," she says. "That's how you learn the basics."

And getting it right was so rewarding. Maria Elisa will never forget the moment when José first lifted the faders (sliding volume controls on the mixing board). The music coming through her headset sounded like a finished album.

After graduation, Maria Elisa did some work producing bands—mixing and recording their music—but that kind of work wasn't easy to get in Colombia. Time and again, upon learning she was female, potential clients would ask, "Can you really produce? Are you actually good at it?"

José knew she was good though. He hired Maria Elisa as the audio postproduction supervisor for the reality TV show *Protagonistas de Nuestra Tele*.

Maria Elisa performed sound design, sound editing, audio mixing, automated dialogue replacement, and sound effects. The film editor completed each day's episode and sent it to her by 2:30 PM on the day it was scheduled to air. That left just five hours, for Maria Elisa to complete all those tasks by showtime—six days a week!

Maria Elisa did TV and film postproduction work in Colombia for four years. She taught too. But she longed to record and mix music, so she applied to a master's program in audio production at Middle Tennessee State University (MTSU). There was only one problem: she didn't have the money for tuition. She had teaching experience though, so MTSU offered her a graduate teaching assistantship, which meant free tuition. Maria Elisa moved to Tennessee.

She got an internship at Creative Caffeine, a Nashville studio owned by Latin percussionist Pino Squillace. On her first day, the studio's engineer quit, so Maria Elisa ran the recording session. Afterward, Pino said, "You're no intern. You're going to be the studio chief now."

Because of her immigration status, being studio chief was an unpaid internship, but the experience was invaluable. At Creative Caffeine, Maria Elisa adopted rigorous professional standards that she still brings to every project.

After completing her master's degree, Maria Elisa needed an employer willing to sponsor her US work visa, so one of her professors recommended her for an assistant position at Criteria Studios in Miami. The job entailed "taking out the trash, preparing fruit bowls, and picking up pizzas for Lil Wayne in the middle of the night," she says. It was a big step down from studio chief, but Maria Elisa didn't mind.

"One thing I'm not afraid of is starting over," she says. "When you're new in town, you're new in town."

Ten days into that job, she received a call from Julio Reyes Copello, one of the top producers of Latin music. Julio had heard about her from a mutual friend. He was producing a record with Il Divo, a world-famous operatic pop quartet. He insisted they meet. Was she available to work the next day?

"Uh, I have a shift at six o'clock at Criteria. I need to take out the garbage," she said.

The next day, he reviewed her demo reel and said, "You're coming to work with me." Maria Elisa quit Criteria.

Her first assignment with Julio was mixing the vocals on the Il Divo album. She soon realized that the hours at a seemingly unrelated job—mixing dialogue in television postproduction—had actually trained her ear for mixing the four distinct singing voices. Julio liked her work and gave her a contract.

In Julio's studio, Maria Elisa did the same kind of recording and mixing work she'd done in Nashville, but for higher-caliber artists. Hearing the voices of Latin pop stars Marc Anthony, J.Lo, Ricky Martin, and Laura Pausini on her headset was awe-inspiring. But she didn't have time to be starstruck. Between June and December of that year, the studio worked on 120 songs.

Maria Elisa describes the art of audio engineering like this:

> In other engineering careers, the science and the math and the numbers won't fail you. With music, you can know all the math in the world, but if the trumpet player has a stomachache, he's not going to be able to blow his trumpet. . . . We have to be really good at the mechanical and technological side of it, but in the end, once you become a good engineer, you forget all of that. And you focus on everything else, everything you can't prepare for—how to deal with musicians and how to

deal with a room and how to deal with weather conditions—things from the performance that have nothing to do with your technology.

When Julio finally took a break, Maria Elisa set up her own studio so she could take private clients between Julio's projects. Those clients include reggaeton artists from Haiti and other parts of the Caribbean. She understands those styles, their roots, and their audiences. "A reggaeton track has to make your chest pump and your hips move," she says.

When colleagues object to the "loudness" in those recordings, Maria Elisa says, "If we don't have loudness in Latin America, we are going to disappoint an entire continent. People are not going to be able to dance."

Around 2017–2018, audio brands began asking Maria Elisa to make demo videos for their products. She also began hosting panels for the Recording Academy in Miami. She was finally using her public speaking skills.

In February 2020, she attended an event for *A Tiny Audience*, where she ran into the show's creator, Maurice Keizer. He'd seen her videos. Would she consider being one of the show's hosts? He wanted viewers to see there was more to the recording industry than just the artists.

In 2021, Maria Elisa signed on as one of three hosts for *A Tiny Audience*'s second season, and Maurice got his wish. The intimate music talk show is recorded live and features acoustic performances just like her childhood favorite, *MTV*

Unplugged. And the regard that *A Tiny Audience*'s famous guests have for the audio engineer comes through in every episode Maria Elisa hosts.

On her birthday in 2021, Maria Elisa listened as the Latin Grammy nominees were announced. Colombian pop star Paula Arenas's *Mis Amores,* an album Maria Elisa produced, engineered, and cowrote, received four nominations: Record of the Year, Album of the Year, Song of the Year ("A Tu Lado"), and Best Traditional Pop Album.

Also nominated was *Ancestras,* a collaborative folklore album featuring 14 powerful Latina vocalists of African descent that Maria Elisa mixed for legendary Afro-Colombian singer-songwriter Petrona Martinez.

"What a birthday present!" she says.

In November, with Maria Elisa in the audience, *Ancestras* won the Latin Grammy for Best Folklore Album. *Mis Amores* did not win a Latin Grammy, but it did receive another accolade—a 2022 Grammy nomination for Best Latin Pop Album.

In April 2022, HBO Latino released season three of *A Tiny Audience* with Maria Elisa hosting seven more episodes. She also mixed and mastered the live music performances for all 16 season-three episodes.

She continues to be busier than ever engineering, recording, and mixing new music. Far too often, young women walk into the recording studio, meet Maria Elisa, and exclaim, "I've never met a woman engineer. That is so cool!"

"This has to stop," says Maria Elisa. The presence of women in audio engineering should be unremarkable. She encourages girls to study STEM and pursue audio production degrees.

In her experience, however, it's still rough going. Women audio engineers typically earn less than their male counterparts, but Maria Elisa is working to change that. In 2021, she was elected to the Recording Academy's National Board of Trustees. She also sits on the Recording Academy Producers and Engineers Wing National Steering Committee. And she continues to teach and mentor new talent.

When time allows, Maria Elisa conducts workshops for aspiring audio engineers in Colombia—either in person or online. Opportunities for female engineers and producers are slowly opening up in her home country and women there are looking to her for leadership.

So, Maria Elisa returns to Colombia to tell her story, and every time, it has an even happier ending.

Sylvia Massy:
Adventure Recording

In search of a sound effect for progressive groove metal band Hydraform's album, music producer Sylvia Massy led the musicians out of the studio. "We need the sound of a cannon, and we don't have a cannon," she explained in a video shot during a recording expedition in the field. Sylvia's tone was quiet and instructive—the voice a guide might use to point out features on the trail ahead. But Sylvia was about to blow up something out there.

Sylvia's enthusiasm for sound—in this case, loud and possibly lethal for mics—might come as a surprise to anyone trained to keep it down. But when she and the band explode Tannerite inside a burn barrel (at the end of the promo clip, which you can find online), it's impossible not to cheer for the cannon-like *BOOM*.

Play the video to the end, and the initial burst of sound dies off, leaving a long wake of satisfying crackling noises.

Sylvia even managed to capture the sound effect without damaging her "lovely" Aston Spirit mic.

"It sounded just like a cannon shot," Sylvia rejoices, "so we used it in the song. But that day of being out in the field, blowing up Tannerite, was something that none of us will ever forget. It was a real bonding experience."

Sylvia Massy is a legendary audio engineer, mixer, and producer with more than three decades of experience and 25-plus gold and platinum records. She's also a visual artist, a published columnist, and an educator who advocates, above all else, for experimentation and rule breaking.

Sylvia lectures everywhere from the Abbey Road Institute and Berklee College of Music to YouTube, where she offers advice that helps music makers open their minds, step out of their boxes, and even blow up a box or two. All this in the interest of creating emotionally powerful and highly original sound.

Sylvia's "Adventure Recording" techniques are experimental in the truest sense—the outcome is uncertain. Her work exemplifies the idea that risk yields reward. And Sylvia is someone who, from an early age, dared to take chances.

Sylvia grew up outside Denver, Colorado, in a home full of music. Her mother sang opera. Her father, a mechanical engineer, listened to classical music on a hi-fi system comprised of equipment he built himself. And young Sylvia?

Despite—or in fact, *because* of—all the "friendly music" in the house, her first album was Alice Cooper's *Killer*. Sylvia was hooked on hard rock, shock rock, glam rock. "It made me smile," she remembers. "It still does today, like as extreme as it can get. I love hard music. And so that's where it started, rebelling against the parents, which is a pretty typical story, I guess."

But Sylvia and her dad had something key in common: a passion for technology. He taught her how to solder, follow signal flow, and fearlessly experiment with mechanical and electrical components. Around age eight, she took an unforgettable trip to a radio station with her father. "I got to see what was going on inside—all the transmitters and the microphones," Sylvia recalls. "And I was fascinated with all that." Little did Sylvia know she was looking into her future.

Back at home, Sylvia commandeered her dad's stereo equipment for her own projects. And one day she made a profound discovery. While listening to Yes's *Fragile* album, she realized that the layers of vocals on "South Side of the Sky" were sung by a single person. "I realized that layering is how you get this effect of all these vocals. One person can do a choir if they just multitrack back and forth between two machines."

Sylvia wouldn't call this "production" until years later, but that didn't slow her down. She began making radio shows, using a cassette machine to record voice and sound effects over silent-movie music played on her father's hi-fi. She even scripted her shows and invited friends to play parts.

Naturally, Sylvia got involved with campus radio production as a college student at California State University, Chico. And broadcasting classes introduced her to professional multitrack recorders, as well as microphones and mixers.

This experience, in turn, translated into a job in radio at Duncan Robertson Productions in Oakland, California. There, she honed her technical skills, experimented with sound, read news, crafted commercials, and adopted scrupulous professional standards for delivering work on time and within budget. But radio's emphasis on ads—instead of music—limited her love for broadcasting.

Eventually, Sylvia took a chance, started knocking on doors, and landed a job running an eight-track studio at Bear West Studios in San Francisco. The change meant a drop in pay, but her job satisfaction went way up.

Meanwhile, Sylvia was fronting the all-girl band Revolver in the San Francisco alt-punk scene. It was the 1980s, and Revolver was playing at all the "hopping" clubs—Mabuhay, On Broadway, the Stone. Their self-produced demos caused a stir. "We would [record] late night, kind of sneaky, maybe," Sylvia recalls. "But some of it came out really good. So people who heard what we were working on asked if I could record them too."

The progression from performer to producer was natural. Sylvia explains, "Just hanging out there, naked basically, in front of people with your music and your emotions is very difficult. And I found myself not as self-confident as a singer and a writer as I was as a producer."

Without a formal education in production or engineering, Sylvia "made it up" as she went along. She'd actually map out music on paper, drawing the curve of "how a song would start and then build and then drop and then build and taper off on the end."

Sylvia's early intuitive approach paid off, and she collaborated with many big Bay Area musicians, including Kirk Hammett from Metallica, with whom she coproduced a record for the Sea Hags. But the San Francisco music scene is small. After five years, Sylvia realized she had to move down to Los Angeles to move up in music production.

Relocating to L.A., with its enormous, established music industry, meant starting over. For two whole years, Sylvia did entry-level work, including retail sales at Tower Records on Sunset Boulevard. But the business of selling records and making records overlapped interestingly in that time and place. Tower Records was a nexus for performing musicians. It's where Sylvia met members of the band Tool, whose music would later change her life.

In 1991, Sylvia finally arrived at her career "crossroads" when she landed a job at Larrabee Sound, a premiere L.A. studio. There, her duties included audio engineering, mixing, producing, and running little errands for big-name artists.

When superstar singer-songwriter Prince came in to record for a few days, one of the first things he wanted was a big chair for his room. Of course, Sylvia offered him one. "But we didn't have one," she recalls. "I lied." To make good on the promise, she had to race out to an antique store.

Prince was impressed by Sylvia's initiative, and she worked on all his sessions. But despite the close conditions, he remained elusive. She remembers, "I was often times guessing and crossing my fingers that I was doing what he wanted." Eventually, that tension broke, but in a most awkward way.

While making the album *Diamonds and Pearls*, Prince wanted to replace music they'd been working on with a song called "Gett Off." Sylvia quietly noted disappointment in her journal: *There's Prince sitting on his purple throne, and he's taking a perfectly good song off of this brilliant record and replacing it with this horrible 'Gett Off' song.*

Later, while helping at the mixing desk, Sylvia heard Prince's voice, "There's Prince sitting on his purple throne." He'd picked up her journal and started reading it aloud!

But instead of anger, Prince expressed amusement. "He thought that was the greatest thing," Sylvia says. "Everyone just gave him lip service constantly, and no one really was honest with him, so I think he was impressed with that. . . . He liked the fact that I had an opinion and it wasn't all positive."

Did experiences like this give Sylvia a sense that she could manage big talent? Not yet. She was living day to day, never knowing who'd be in the studio. She was always on call, pulling all-nighters, hoping those extra hours would make the difference. And she gambled on unpaid side jobs just to get experience in different genres.

But there was one thing she could not risk in those years:

I was going from working at Tower Records to working in the studio with big stars. And I had to make a decision about my sobriety. To be honest, I love to party. And I had to make a decision right there. Do I want to keep partying, or do I want to get serious about my career? And so, I quit everything. . . . I quit smoking. . . quit drinking. . . . Done. And what happened was astounding because, in that first year of sobriety, all this opportunity flooded to me.

And Sylvia was ready for it.

At Larrabee, she worked with stars like Paula Abdul, Aerosmith, and Julio Iglesias, and she did several projects with Prince, whose *Diamonds and Pearls* album earned a multiplatinum certification.

When offered an opportunity to move to Paisley Park, Prince's production complex, Sylvia turned it down. Instead, she followed her heart into hard music production for Tool's extended play (EP) *Opiate*, which went platinum, and their debut studio album, *Undertow*, which went multiplatinum.

Along with famed producer Rick Rubin, Sylvia worked on the heavy metal band System of a Down's debut album, hip-hop band Geto Boys' debut, rocker Tom Petty and the Heartbreakers' *She's the One*, Red Hot Chili Peppers' "Love Rollercoaster," and Johnny Cash's album *Unchained*, which won a Grammy Award for Best Country Album.

The World of Producers According to Sylvia

- **Engineer/producer:** This is the person, like Sylvia, who understands the equipment and uses it as a tool to help clients realize their musical goals. Nigel Godrich, well known for his work with Radiohead, is an engineer/producer.
- **Musician/producer:** In this role, producers create songs and partner with musicians to perform them. The duo Nova Wav shines a light on this work in chapter 13. Though Sylvia doesn't generally write parts, she'll add them if necessary.
- **Fan/producer:** Everyone has a bit of fan/producer in them, but Rick Rubin is the example par excellence. He's not a technician or musician. Instead, he listens and asks questions: Does this song have a hook? Will it appeal to its audience? How can we make it better? Sylvia likes playing the fan/producer too. And if she engineers at the same time, that gives her a lot of control.

For a longer look at producers, check out *Recording Unhinged*, where Sylvia and coauthor Chris Johnson reimagine recording industry heroes as mythological gods.

Sylvia struck out on her own in 2001. Her first stop was the Weed Palace Theater in Northern California where she owned and operated RadioStar Studios, serving international musicians such as reggae and ska band Sublime, Australian progressive rock band Cog, and From First to Last, featuring Sonny Moore of Skrillex.

As of 2012, Sylvia has run a private studio in Ashland, Oregon, working with all-women noise band Thunderpussy, Persian rapper Chaii, Mexican rockers Molotov, and late Foo Fighter drummer Taylor Hawkins, to name a few.

When she's not producing music, Sylvia speaks about it and supports young artists through initiatives like the Sylvia Massy Scholarship, which is awarded to music production students at the Academy of Contemporary Music. She's also widely celebrated as a woman who paves the way for others.

"It's harder for women," she explains. You don't see as many women in the industry because many are making hard choices related to family-building. "As much as we want to have equality, we're having babies. We get to do that." Sylvia encourages young women to think about that challenging time, maybe ten years into a career, when it might be necessary to pause to focus on motherhood.

Or not, of course. Sylvia chose not to have children, and she leads "a very fulfilled life."

Sylvia's partner, Chris Johnson, an accomplished writer and the steady hand behind Sylvia's career, describes her extraordinary character and achievements like this: "A big part of her success has been simply being who she is, and not bending to the pressure to be something else."

A lot has changed since Sylvia stood at the "crossroads" of her career. Now she selects her own clients and sets her own schedule. But she hasn't grown averse to risk over the years. In fact, she experiments more than ever. "Music is emotion," she says. "Every song is an adventure into someone's soul."

When a client comes into the studio with a new project, she's ready to play a variety of roles. "Sometimes I write arrangements, sing backing tracks, hire players, completely rework the songs . . . and sometimes I am simply a cheerleader." And if the song doesn't call for cheer, Sylvia isn't afraid to make artists uncomfortable.

"Let's say you're doing music that's angry," she explains. "You want to have the singer *with* that anger—true anger in their voice—well, then you just have to piss them off." To that end, she might send a musician out of the studio to run around in the snow (as she did with the vocalist of Norwegian band Seigmen) or hang upside down (like System of a Down's singer). The idea is to act now, apologize later.

Working like this requires a tolerance for rejection. Sylvia comes up with more ideas than clients accept. But her job is to help artists realize *their* goals. She has her own creative outlets, including visual art. That's her "pure expression." Sylvia channels a lot of music into her visuals. It's there in illustrations drawn for her books and large canvas paintings created while recording in the studio or laying over in a hotel.

Travel is essential for an adventure recorder since location can profoundly affect performance. Imagine recording vocals in an insulated studio room versus a soaring cathedral. Sylvia sets aside one day in a session (usually the last) to do something "outrageous," like recording in a church, castle, or cave. The outcome is always uncertain but never disappointing.

With the band Machines of Loving Grace, Sylvia created a sacrificial guitar—a 50-dollar instrument that musicians were prepared to part with. Everyone adorned it with carvings, paintings, and parting wishes before throwing it over a cliff in Malibu! They got a great feedback tone going just before the drop and recorded the tumble down with a long instrument cable connected to a recording rig at the top.

But, alas, fans never heard the glorious cacophony of noise captured that day. "We tried it everywhere in the album," Sylvia laments, "and it just didn't work."

If you, too, are thinking that's a terrible shame, then you just might be an adventure recorder. But don't fret about the deceased guitar—it didn't die in vain. The instrument was framed and hung in a studio control room, and it will live on in story. "No one will ever forget the experience of tossing that guitar," she says.

So take it from Sylvia: make your recordings an adventure. "That way, you'll walk away with memories you'll never lose."

Studio Museum

Microphones are embedded in much of the modern world, but sound transmission was not possible just 150 years ago. As curators of the world's largest collection of vintage mics (2,500-plus), Sylvia and Chris are uniquely poised to give a tour of the world of recording.

Wondering how to plug in an oldie?

Well, the 1878 mic in the collection consists of two posts on the ends of a carbon pencil (basically a burned stick). If you run a current through it (from a battery) and talk into it, the variable resistance is translated through the wire and into a speaker. This is an early version of technology that later became ubiquitous—most landline phones had a carbon button in the mouthpiece.

While that's an example of "yelling at a stick," you can "holler at a rock" too. In a crystal mic, sound energy vibrates a thin wafer of crystal which, in turn, puts out a little charge that results in an audio signal.

The collection also contains examples of delicate ribbon mics and high-fidelity condenser mics and, of course, trusty dynamic mics.

If you're brand new to studio work, Sylvia recommends picking up a dynamic mic, like a Shure SM 58, because it's good for a range of sound. And she wishes you happy recording!

Tribute to Sophie Xeon

During the writing of this book, a potential interviewee, Sophie Xeon, stage name SOPHIE, died after an accidental fall from a balcony in Athens, Greece. SOPHIE was thirty-four years old, a rising superstar in the world of experimental pop, and an unapologetic force for change in the music industry.

SOPHIE's vision for the future of music was unequivocal. "It should be mind-blowing! Every single thing you hear should feel like you've never heard something like that before. Like it makes you feel alive in a new way. Like it makes you feel reborn." In little more than a decade as a professional, SOPHIE ran hard at this goal, producing a sound that listeners could only describe as SOPHIE-esque.

SOPHIE, who preferred not to use gendered or nonbinary pronouns, came out as a trans woman during the *Oil of Every Pearl's Un-Insides* tour. This chapter is a tribute to an artist who inspired a generation of LGBTQ+ club kids.

SOPHIE's love affair with music began during childhood in 1990s Scotland. Though not a creative himself, SOPHIE's father envisioned an electronic future. "He had brilliant instincts," SOPHIE recalled. "He bought me . . . rave cassette tapes before I went to the events and would play them in the car and be like, 'This is going to be important for you.'"

He couldn't have been more right. SOPHIE stole those tapes from the car, listened obsessively, and decided to quit school to become an electronic music producer. Alas, that was out of the question for a nine-year-old. But instruments and equipment started trickling into the house, including a birthday guitar and secondhand recording tech from a family friend. By age 14, SOPHIE was telling people, "When I get home from school, I'm just going to lock myself in my room until I've made an album."

The bedroom recording booth became a refuge. "Music, I suppose, became my escape, like this friend I was looking for that was about the same stuff as me," SOPHIE explained. "I filtered a lot of my energy into music to process stuff, and to have a place where I could be alone with my thoughts— whether that's anger, disappointment."

In listening to SOPHIE's body of work, "this energy can be felt," wrote journalist Ivan Guzman. But what's harder for writers and fans to perceive is the source. Does SOPHIE's music flow from a place of happiness? Sorrow? Something else?

SOPHIE experimented endlessly with synthesized sound, eventually letting a brother into the booth to help. "We'll just sit there designing little music instruments, essentially," SOPHIE remembered. "It's like if you're with your best friend, and there's a bunch of clay there in the middle. And you're like, oh, imagine if we twist it a bit here, imagine if we put this edge on it, imagine if we colored it this color. . . . You're just using your ears, and the sounds are directly speaking to your emotions."

Communicating vulnerability through noise and voice—that was SOPHIE's superpower. And SOPHIE wielded it at both the experimental fringe of electronic dance music and in the center of the pop world, recording with stars such as Kim Petras, Charli XCX, and Madonna in the 2010s.

SOPHIE remained largely out of the public eye until 2018, when the music video for "It's Okay to Cry" was released. With that, explains writer Harrison Brocklehurst, SOPHIE went from "elusive underground artist" to one who told fans that "being trans was something to own, something to celebrate and something to be fearless with."

SOPHIE's debut album, *Oil of Every Pearl's Un-Insides*, earned a Grammy nomination in 2019 for Best Dance/Electronic Album.

The impact of SOPHIE's work will be discussed for years to come, including the question of where all that hyperpop energy flowed from—a happy place? Sad? Angsty?

SOPHIE's answer: confused. "The main feeling for me is just being overwhelmed at the ridiculousness and complexity of the world we live in and how difficult it is to comprehend."

Perhaps that's why SOPHIE's music resonates so strongly—why it has the power to "blow people's minds with possibility."

Coda

Nothing moves us like music. In *Music Mavens*, you've traveled the world—and beyond—to a jazz performance in Genoa, an instrument lab in London, a Tokyo taiko dojo, a New York City beatbox battle, and even a film-scoring session aboard the starship *Enterprise*. Along the way, you met seventeen artists whose work spans a range of musical genres and industry roles. Today, they're women of note. But they were once beginners like many of you. Their journeys began with a single step—one you can take anytime.

Think of that place—early in the creative process—where music is composed, a score is arranged, and lyrics are written. The relationship between the sound and the page is what orchestrator Macy Schmidt loves most. Film composer Nami Melumad also revels in the score, explaining that with film music "you can write music and you can tell a story too." Is there a song you're burning to write? Go for it.

Kate Schutt describes the allure of the singer-songwriter role like this: "I play music because it connects me to awe and wonder."

If you, too, are a singer, consider joining a choir. "When we are together, we're strong," says conductor Valérie Sainte-Agathe. But don't forget the brave examples of Janet Dacal, who started her career singing solo in a stairwell, and Kaila Mullady, who found her jam beatboxing solo on street corners. For the instrumentalists out there, Regina Carter and Vân-Ánh Vanessa Võ show how classical and traditional training go hand in hand with improvisation. And free-spirited percussionist Kaoly Asano reveals the truly transformative power of connecting with an audience.

Beyond performance, there's the place in the song life cycle where music is recorded and produced. That's where sound engineer Maria Elisa Ayerbe combines music with STEM. It's where power duo Nova Wav thrives, writing and producing hits for superstars. As Sylvia Massy demonstrates, the role of producer can be an adventure. Her dare: to "unlearn" safe record-making, stick your head out the sunroof, and put the pedal to the metal!

You can experience more of these artists' work by visiting the playlist at the back of this book. There, you can also explore artist-recommended resources for aspiring musicians, such as classes and networking opportunities. And be sure to visit the book's website, www.musicmavensbook.com, where you'll find news, photos, and links to music.

If any of these women perform in your town, don't miss the show. Remember multidisciplinary artist Lia Mice's parting words: "They love music, I love music, so, of course, we can be friends."

Ovation

When we set out to write *Music Mavens*, we didn't expect to travel the globe. But it's been a thrill to take trips to studios and stages around the world, and we're grateful to the crew of incredible people who made this adventure possible.

First, our gratitude goes to the women who shared their stories. They rearranged schedules packed with rehearsals, tours, recording dates, and teaching to speak with us. And they spoke candidly. Sometimes the interviews came with laughter, sometimes tears, but always with deep authenticity. Thanks to these artists for sharing personal highs and lows and professional dos and don'ts to inspire and educate young readers.

Support from the music community didn't stop there, though. Thanks, also, to those who helped behind the scenes. We're talking about busy industry people who found time to introduce us to a big star or answer little tech questions: How does an audio sampler work? Can you tune a taiko drum? What's a nova? We're grateful to the following generous and knowledgeable experts: Monina Sen Cervone, Kev Choice, John Clayton, Dr. Susan Helfter, Hunter Payne, Elauna Samuels, Faelan Westhead, Dr. Chris Wipf, Aya Yoshida, and the American Society of Music Arrangers and Composers. We've also benefitted from the extraordinary music teachers in our own lives. Maureen wishes to acknowledge choral directors Joanne Perez, Sister Oliver, Sister Damian, Father John Mayhew, Father Rick Abert, and Linda Silbert, and guitar teachers Marcia Fuller and Kelsey Walker. Ashley is grateful for Lynn and Roy Oakley and Julie Smolin at the Villa Sinfonia Foundation, James Moore at Green Room Music, Monina Sen Cervone at the Ruth Asawa School of the Arts, and Vân-Ánh Vanessa Võ at the Au Co Vietnamese Cultural Center.

Every book project—even one with such glamorous content as this—involves the day-to-day work of an author, and we're thanking our lucky stars for our literary team. Agent extraordinaire Kelly Dyksterhouse steered us through the contracts to get the book cleared for takeoff. Smart, organized, and talented, Kelly also helped us revise the book proposal until it, too, sang! And we couldn't have asked for a better editor than Kara Rota. She commented on early, mid, and final drafts with insight and focus that landed the book beyond our highest hopes. Thanks to Kara Rota and the other brilliant people working at and with Chicago Review Press, especially project editor Ben Krapohl, copyeditor Christine Florie, cover designer and illustrator Sadie Teper, and the typesetters at Nord Compo.

Our writing lives would be far less interesting and productive without a lively village of author friends. We're thankful for their support during the creation of this book and always. These dear critique partners, accountability partners, and authenticity readers include Finnlay Alexander, Rebecca Birkin, Stephani Eaton, Marisilda Garcia, Shira Graff, Jennifer Kay, Tamika Lamison, Sharon Langley, Andrea Loney, Lindsey Manwell, DoanPhuong Nguyen, Katrina O'Gilvie, Manisha Patel, Sue Schmitt, Diane Telgen, and Whitney Walker.

We also extend our thanks to the brilliant faculty and staff of Vermont College of Fine Arts (VCFA), where we both earned MFAs in writing for children and young adults. Without VCFA, we would have never met, never collaborated on a book, and never had the tools and know-how to make this book beautiful.

Last, but never least, we're grateful to our local people.

Ashley wishes to thank her family, Martin Westhead and kids, for inspiration, understanding, and homecooked dinners during the long work-at-home year that was 2021. I'm so lucky to have your laughter in the soundtrack of my life.

Maureen thanks her son Shakib for his boundless love and support and her late husband—arranger, orchestrator, and composer Jon Charles—for 24 years of joyful harmony. You two inspired every word.

Playlist

Note: Songs from the albums listed can be found on Spotify and most other music streaming services. You can find a longer linked playlist at www.musicmavensbook.com.

Kaoly Asano

"Quest" on *Ancient River*
GOCOO live in concert at the 2015 Paléo Festival Nyon on YouTube
GOCOO Mizu no Codoo on YouTube
"Teahouse" and "Tetsujin," recorded with Juno Reactor, for *The Matrix Reloaded* and *The Matrix Revolutions* movies
Finding Her Beat documentary at www.herbeatfilm.com

Maria Elisa Ayerbe

A Tiny Audience, seasons two and three (12 episodes hosted by Maria Elisa), on HBO Max
"A Tu Lado" on Paula Arenas's *Mis Amores*
"El Piano de Dolores y Estefanía" on Petrona Martínez's *Ancestras*
"Mantra" on Rosa Rosa's *La Flor de La Verdad*
Mixed by Maria Elisa Ayerbe multitrack Spotify list

Katarina Benzova

"Music" at Katarina Benzova's website, www.katbenzova.com
"Media" at Guns N' Roses' website, www.gunsnroses.com
"Katarina Benzova" at the Rock Photography Museum website, www
.rockphotographymuseum.com/product-category/katarina-benzova/
"Campaigns" at Mission 11's website, www.mission11.org
"One Golden Thread Badassador Kat Benzova" at onegoldenthread.com
/blogs/badassadors/katerina-benzova-mission11

Regina Carter

"Cinema Paradiso" on *Paganini After a Dream*
"I'm Going Home" on *Southern Comfort*
"Oh, Lady Be Good!" on *Rhythms of the Heart*
Regina Carter: NPR Music Tiny Desk Concert on YouTube
"Softly, As in a Morning Sunrise" with Kenny Barron on *Freefall*

Janet Dacal

"Don't Cry for Me Argentina" on *Prince of Broadway* (Cast Recording)
"Happier Than the Morning Sun . . . Lin's Wedding Surprise," *In the Heights* cast performs at Lin-Manuel Miranda's wedding on YouTube
"It Don't Mean a Thing" on Janet Dacal's *My Standards*
"No Me Diga" on the *In the Heights* (Original Broadway Cast Recording)
"Omar Sharif" video of Janet from *The Band's Visit National Tour* on YouTube

Sylvia Massy

The World's Largest Microphone Collection at www.sylviamassy.com
Recording Unhinged: Creative and Unconventional Music Recording Techniques by Sylvia Massy with Chris Johnson (book)
"Digibasse" featuring B Wise on Chaii's *Lightswitch* EP (mix)
"Strangers" on Selci's *Effervescence* EP (mix)
"Ghost" featuring Prince and Kate Bush at www.sylviamassy.com/music (engineer)

Nami Melumad

An American Pickle, feature film starring Seth Rogen, on HBO Max
Luminarias, five-minute short on Catherine Choolijian's Vimeo channel
"New Zealand's Guide to Tessering" on YouTube
Over the Wall, short film by Roy Zafrani, at www.omeleto.com
Star Trek Prodigy and *Star Trek: Strange New Worlds* series on Paramount+

Lia Mice

"Sweat Like Caramel" on *Sweat Like Caramel*
"Which Memories Will Make It" on *The Sampler as a Time Machine*
Score for the psychological thriller *A Quiet Room in Walthamstow*
One-Handed Violin documentary at www.liamice.com
Tasogare documentary at www.liamice.com

Kaila Mullady

"Beatboxing 101 with Kaila" on YouTube (tutorial)
"Kaila Mullady—Legends Live in Studio Performance" on YouTube
"Kaila Mullady Showcase, Long Island Beatbox Battle 2019" on YouTube
"World Beatboxing Champion Kaila Mullady" on YouTube
"Yodel Meet Auctioneer—Full Film" Gap commercial on YouTube

Nova Wav

"Black Parade" on Beyoncé's *The Lion King: The Gift* (cowriters)
"Commitment" on Monica's *Chapter 38* album (producers, cowriters)
"CRZY" on Kehlani's *SweetSexySavage* album (producers, cowriters)
"LoveHappy" on the Carters's *Everything Is Love* album (cowriters)
"Pick Up Your Feelings" on Jazmine Sullivan's *Heaux Tales* (cowriters)

Valérie Sainte-Agathe

"Hallelujah" with The King's Singers at www.sfgirlschorus.org
Rightfully Ours with Berkeley Ballet Theater at www.sfgirlschorus.org

Music With Changing Parts with the Philip Glass Ensemble at www
.sfgirlschorus.org

"Music of Spheres" with the Kronos Quartet and the Afghanistan National
Music Institute students on *Final Answer*

"Panda Chant" composed by Meredith Monk at TEDxSanFrancisco

Macy Schmidt

The Broadway Sinfonietta YouTube videos featuring Macy's orchestrations:

"Here Comes the Change, Inauguration Eve" (feat. Shoba Narayan)

"It Starts with Me" (feat. Lianah Sta. Ana)

Ratatouille: The TikTok Musical, soundtrack on the official Ratatouille The
Musical YouTube channel

"Summertime" by Women of Color on Broadway, Inc.

"You're Gonna Hear from Me" (feat. Solea Pfeiffer)

Kate Schutt

"A Grief Casserole—How to Help Your Friends and Family Through Loss,"
Kate's TEDx West Chester talk on YouTube

"How Much In Love" on *No Love Lost*

"Roll the Stone Back" on *Bright Nowhere*

"Take Everything" on *Telephone Game*

"Wrecking Ball" on *No Love Lost*

Joanne Shenandoah

"Kahawi'tha" on *Matriarch*

"Prophecy Song" on *Orenda*

Skywoman, a pop-orchestral production of an Iroquois Creation Story

"Seeking the Light" on *Sacred Ground: A Tribute to Mother Earth*

"Treaty" on *Eagle Cries*

Vân-Ánh Vanessa Võ

Soundtrack to *The People vs. Agent Orange*

"Purple Haze," a đàn bầu cover of Jimi Hendrix's classic on YouTube

"Summertime" with Nguyen Le at *National Public Radio Classical*

"Three-Mountain Pass" on *Three-Mountain Pass*

"Van-Anh Vanessa: Vo Tiny Desk Concert" on the National Public Radio YouTube channel

Resources

Are you a songwriter or rapper? Do you dream of conducting? Ever wonder where to meet aspiring record producers or audio engineers? Start your search here, with pointers to industry and educational resources. You can find more details, including a linked resource list, at www.music mavensbook.com.

American Society of Music Arrangers and Composers promotes the art of music arranging, composition, and orchestration.

Drake Music is a leading organization in the United Kingdom that strives to create an inclusive environment for musicians with disabilities.

Geri Allen Jazz Camp is a week-long residency (on-site or virtual) for female-identifying or nonbinary performers (ages 14-26) led by Regina Carter and a distinguished faculty of jazz musicians.

Girls Make Beats hosts educational seminars, summer camps, industry panels, and networking events for girls ages 5–17 to help further their careers as music producers, DJs, and audio engineers.

The Hiawatha Institute of Indigenous Knowledge, cofounded by Joanne Shenandoah, brings Iroquois cultural knowledge to the world.

kaDON is the US branch of Miyamoto Unosuke Shoten and a subscription-based online taiko and fue (Japanese drum and flute) learning platform with a growing library of downloadable play-along tracks, exercises, and scores. Kaoly Asano teaches for kaDON.

Luna Composition Lab provides mentorship and performance opportunities.

Los Angeles Inception Orchestra infuses music education with composition, orchestration, and music theory.

Mission11, founded by Katarina Benzova, provides complimentary campaign design, photography, and cinematography to organizations combating Earth's challenges.

Mr. Holland's Opus Foundation donates high-quality musical instruments to deserving, under-funded music programs.

Music Bridge, supported by Vân-Ánh Vanessa Võ, is a Vietnamese American nongovernmental organization program for young artists studying traditional music.

The One-Handed Musical Instrument Trust, through which Lia Mice built her one-handed violin, enables musicians with physical impairments to take part in music making.

In *Recording Unhinged: Creative and Unconventional Music Recording Techniques*, authors Sylvia Massy and Chris Johnson dare you to "put the pedal to the metal" with adventurous recording techniques.

The Rock Photography Museum preserves, promotes, and presents the photographic legacy of rock and roll.

San Francisco Girls Chorus and Artistic Director Valérie Sainte-Agathe prepare girls for success, on stage and in life, through rigorous, empowering music education.

She Is the Music, founded by Alicia Keys, is dedicated to increasing the number of women working in music.

Soundgirls supports women working in professional audio engineering and music production.

TAWOO is an organization produced by GOCOO, whose four pillars include performance activities, taiko dojo, taiko workshop, and a taiko program for children.

We Are Moving the Needle is a nonprofit organization supporting female recording industry professionals.

Women in Music advances equality, diversity, and opportunities for women in the musical arts through education, support, and recognition.

Notes

Prelude

Every known human culture: Daniel J. Levitin, *This Is Your Brain on Music: The Science of a Human Obsession* (New York: Dutton, 2007), 238–245.

"You are transported": *Music, Sound and the Sacred with Joanne Shenandoah and Alan Jones*, directed by Stephen Olsson (Global Spirit, CEM Productions, 2016), http://www.globalspirit.tv/project/music-sound -and-the-sacred/.

1. Macy Schmidt: Orchestrating Equity

"I have chills": Ashley Lee, Twitter post by @cashleelee, January 1, 2021.

"I am LIVING": Tay, Twitter post by @KingTaylo_, January 1, 2021.

"not because they": All quotes from an author interview with Macy Schmidt on September 15, 2021, unless otherwise noted.

"an all female-identifying": "Home Page," The Broadway Sinfonietta official website, accessed May 10, 2022, https://www.thebroadway sinfonietta.com.

"I had about": Julia Reinstein, "How 'Ratatouille' Went from TikTok to an (Almost) Broadway Musical," *BuzzFeed*, January 2, 2021, https:// www.buzzfeednews.com/article/juliareinstein/ratatouille-musical -tiktok-broadway.

"classic Disney": Jesse Green, "'Ratatouille' Review: What's Small and Hairy with Big Dreams?" *New York Times*, January 3, 2021.

Notes

2. Lia Mice: Innovating Inclusion

"Just always": Sam Davies, "'We Need to Put Inclusion at the Start of the Process': The Disabled Musicians Making Their Own Instruments," *Guardian*, July 10, 2019.

"Music saved my life": Davies, "We Need to Put."

"When I'm in control": All quotes from an author interview with Lia Mice on April 21, 2021, unless otherwise noted.

"I was constantly": "Exploring Sound, Time, and Samples with Lia Mice," Selekta.fm, November 2018, https://www.selekta.fm/lia-mice/.

"I still remember": *Tasogare*, directed by Lia Mice (Vimeo, 2016), https://www.liamice.com.

The festival's name: *Tasogare*, directed by Lia Mice (Vimeo, 2016), https://www.liamice.com.

"Lia Mice makes": Ross Devlin, "Lia Mice—'Tasogare,'" *Tiny Mix Tapes*, December 23, 2016, https://www.tinymixtapes.com/chocolate-grinder/premiere-lia-mice-tasogare.

A 2017 UK study: "Women in Tech: Time to Close the Gender Gap." *PwC*, March 2017, https://www.pwc.co.uk/women-in-technology/womenin-tech-report.pdf.

3. Katarina Benzova: Shooting Stars

"there are moments": Katarina Benzova official website, accessed May 11, 2022, https://www.katbenzova.com.

"I discovered a talent": All quotes are from an author interview on September 19, 2021, unless otherwise noted.

"I think my dreams": Leslie Michele Derrough, "Rock Photographer Katarina Benzova Shares Her Story," *Glide Magazine*, January 12, 2015, https://glidemagazine.com/129090/rock-photograher-katarina-benzova-shares-story-interview/.

"You are circled": Derrough, "Rock Photographer."

"She got the best": Stacie Vanaga, "Guns N' Roses Tour Photographer, Scuba Diver, and Animal Advocate, Katarina Benzova," *Salted Spirit* podcast, May 15, 2020, https://saltedspirit.libsyn.com/guns-n-roses-tour-photographer-scuba-diver-animal-advocate.

"After the concert": Matthias Dadpreneur Hombauer, "Katarina Benzova: Touring with Guns N' Roses and AC/DC," *How to Become a Rockstar Photographer (HTBARP)* podcast, May 1, 2017, https://www.howtobecomearockstarphotographer.com/podcast-katarina-benzova/.

day in the life of a tour photographer: Hombauer, "Katarina Benzova."

"*Everything was the same*": Derrough, "Rock Photographer."

"*like lightning rods*": Katarina Benzova official website.

"*I've seen a million*": Katarina Benzova official website.

"*one of the best*": Katarina Benzova official website.

"*That was the biggest honor*": Derrough, "Rock Photographer."

"*I've been on the road*": "Meet Katarina Benzova, Music/Documentary Photographer," *ShoutLA*, August 10, 2020, https://shoutoutla.com /meet-katarina-benzova-music-documentary-photographer/.

"*Don't be afraid*": Hombauer, "Katarina Benzova."

4. Janet Dacal: Hitting Broadway Heights

"*Having that in*": All quotes are from an author interview with Janet Dacal on August 9, 2021, unless otherwise noted.

"*In the middle*": Josh Ferri, "Janet Dacal Takes On Seven Questions About *Prince of Broadway*, Evita, Chita, and More!" Broadwaybox, October 17, 2017, https://www.broadwaybox.com/daily-scoop/seven-questions -with-prince-of-broadway-star-janet-dacal/.

5. Valérie Sainte-Agathe: Stronger Together

"*When we are together*": San Francisco Girls Chorus official website, accessed May 11, 2022, https://www.sfgirlschorus.org/.

"*It's about trusting*": Voices of Music, "Women Music Directors: Chloe Kim, Rachel Podger, Valérie Sainte-Agathe and Hanneke van Proosdij," YouTube, November 27, 2020, https://www.youtube.com/watch?v= YoUpaXovceY.

"*It was a beautiful project*": All quotes are from an author interview with Valérie Sainte-Agathe on August 26, 2021, unless otherwise noted.

"*we need to be careful*": The King's Singers, "Workshop with Valérie Sainte-Agathe (The King's Singers New Music Prize)," YouTube, August 22, 2020, https://www.youtube.com/watch?v=t07zmbziE7o.

"*I took the time*": Lisa Houston, "Listening to the Moment: Valérie Sainte-Agathe Leads the SF Girls Chorus Through Unusual Times," *SF Classical Voice*, June 29, 2020, https://www.sfcv.org/articles/artist -spotlight/listening-moment-valerie-sainte-agathe-leads-sf-girls -chorus-through.

"*I think it's only*": Houston, "Listening to the Moment."

Notes

6. Kaoly Asano: Soul, Spirit, and Sound

"I'm finally back": All quotes are from an author interviews with Kaoly Asano in July 2021, unless otherwise noted.

"Your heart is a taiko": Associated Press, "Daihachi Oguchi, 84, Japanese Drummer, Dies," *New York Times,* June 28, 2008, https://www.nytimes.com/2008/06/28/arts/music/28oguchi.html.

"100 Japanese people who overcame": *Newsweek Japan,* July 8, 2009.

7. Nami Melumad: Cinematic Scoring

"There's a spotting": All quotes from an author interview with Nami Melumad on August 21, 2021, unless otherwise noted.

"I'm always fascinated": Tim Greiving, "Rachel Portman Steps Away from the Screen with 'Ask the River,'" NPR, May 21, 2020, https://www.npr.org/2020/05/21/854974173/rachel-portman-steps-away-from-the-screen-with-ask-the-river.

"It's the director" and *"You have no"*: "ASMAC Celebrating Women Composers: Nami Melumad, Nerida Tyson-Chew, and Macy Schmidt," American Society of Music Arrangers and Composers, video event, livestreamed March 6, 2021.

"Rogen plays both": Amon Warmann, "Nami Melumad on Scoring 'An American Pickle,'" *Composer Magazine-Spitfire Audio,* n.d.

"So I wrote": Warmann, "Nami Melumad."

8. Joanne Shenandoah: Standing in Power

"My family always": Anne Desgranges, "An Interview with Joanne Shenandoah." *Cultural Survival,* June 2000, https://www.culturalsurvival.org/publications/cultural-survival-quarterly/interview-joanne-shenandoah.

"They taught the young men": J. Poet, "Joanne Shenandoah: A Singing Spirit," reprinted with permission from *Indian Artists,* accessed July 6, 2021, https://www.hanksville.org/jpoet/shenandoah.html.

"Every word we speak": Marisa Arbona-Ruiz, "Musician Joanne Shenandoah, a Powerful Voice for Native Culture, Dies at 64," NPR, November 27, 2021, https://www.npr.org/2021/11/27/1059526800/musician-joanne-shenandoah-a-powerful-voice-for-native-culture-dies-at-64.

"What amazed me": Matt Schudel, "Joanne Shenandoah, Indigenous Singer of Majestic Lyricism, Dies at 64," *Washington Post,* December 5, 2021, https://www.washingtonpost.com/obituaries/2021/12/05/joanne-shenandoah-dies/.

Notes

"My grandma was": This and all subsequent quotes are from an author interview with Joanne Shenandoah on June 14, 2021, unless otherwise noted.

"I was working": Brenna Sanchez, "Joanne Shenandoah Biography," *Musician Guide*, accessed June 20, 2021, https://musicianguide.com/biographies /1608002995/Joanne-Shenandoah.html.

"I knew I": *Dancing on Mother Earth*, directed by Jim Virga, produced by Tula Goenka, National PBS Special, 2002.

"There was": Doug George-Kanentiio, "On the Life and Death of My Wife Joanne Shenandoah," *IndianZ*, December 6, 2021, https://www .indianz.com/News/2021/12/06/doug-george-kanentiio-on-my-journey -with-joanne-shenandoah/.

"Every breath": Arbona-Ruiz, "Musician Joanne Shenandoah."

"the good mind": Matt Schudel, "Joanne Shenandoah."

"She weaves": Arbona-Ruiz, "Musician Joanne Shenandoah."

"When I create music": *Music, Sound and the Sacred with Joanne Shenandoah and Alan Jones*, directed by Stephen Olsson (Global Spirit, CEM Productions, 2016), http://www.globalspirit.tv/project/music-sound -and-the-sacred/.

"These things are": Desgranges, "An Interview with Joanne Shenandoah."

"Winning and bringing": Sanchez, "Joanne Shenandoah Biography."

"This is what I do": Oswego State University of New York Arts and Culture News, "Grammy-Winning Joanne Shenandoah to Help Open Global Awareness Conference," November 3, 2020, https:// www.oswego.edu/news/story/grammy-winning-joanne-shenan doah-help-open-global-awareness-conference.

"Her light and beauty": Doug George-Kanentiio and Leah Shenandoah, "Joanne Shenandoah—Words of Kanentiio Doug George & Leah Shenandoah on Her Legacy," YouTube, December 8, 2021, https:// www.youtube.com/watch?v=zWVEpaDyX20.

9. Kate Schutt: Presence Not Perfection

"Presence not perfection": All quotes are from an author interview with Kate Schutt on November 9, 2021, unless otherwise noted.

"I can't imagine": Kate Schutt, "You More Than Me," *Bright Nowhere* album, 2021. Used with permission.

"Death come slow": Kate Schutt, "Death Come Slow," *Bright Nowhere* album, 2021. Used with permission.

"I know you": Kate Schutt, "Nothing I Won't Bear," *Bright Nowhere* album, 2021. Used with permission.

"I always go": Rebecca Haslam, "Interviews: Kate Schutt Talks 'Death Come Slow' and 'Bright Nowhere,'" *PopWrapped*, January 5, 2021, https://popwrapped.com/kate-schutt-death-come-slow-bright-nowhere/.

"He had the chops": Haslam, "Interviews: Kate Schutt."

"one of the best": John Apice, "Review: Kate Schutt 'Bright Nowhere' Is Faithful and Sad," *Americana Highways*, April 28, 2021, https://americanahighways.org/2021/04/28/review-kate-schutt-bright-nowhere-is-faithful-and-sad/.

10. Kaila Mullady: Beatboxing Brilliance

"It's impossible for": All quotes from an author interview with Kaila Mullady on January 29, 2021, unless otherwise noted.

"a biracial queer woman" and *"to empower and"*: "About Butterscotch," Butterscotch official website, accessed December 17, 2021, https://butterscotchmusic.com/about/.

"to help people": "Home Page," The Academy of Noise official website, accessed April 21, 2022, https://www.theacademyofnoise.com.

"practices being nervous": Seth Marcus, "Kaila Mullady: The Habits of a Beatboxing World Champion," *The MindMill*, episode 42, July 8, 2019, https://themindmill.com/kaila-mullady/.

11. Vân-Ánh Vanessa Võ: Tradition and Improvisation

86,400 challenge: Asian Women of Power Leader Anhlan Nguyen (https://www.dranhlan.com) posed this scenario.

"86,400": Vietnamese lyrics by Vân-Ánh Vanessa Võ and English lyrics by Kev Choice from *Songs of Strength*. Used with permission.

"drop by drop": All quotes are from an author interview with Vân-Ánh Vanessa Võ on February 9, 2021, unless otherwise noted.

mere bike ride: Jeremy Geffen, "Artist Conversation with Vân-Ánh Vanessa Võ," *Cal Performances*, December 4, 2021, https://calperformances.org/related-events/artist-conversation-with-van-anh-vo-2021-22-season/.

a role that: American Composers Forum, "One Sheet Review: Vân-Ánh Võ 'Three Mountain Pass,'" *Innova Recording Catalog*, September 24, 2013, https://www.innova.mu/albums/van-anh-vanessa-vo/three-mountain-pass.

"One of my": Andrew Lam, "The Odyssey—From Vietnam to America: An Interview with Vân-Ánh Võ," DVAN, February 22, 2016, https://dvan

Notes

.org/2016/02/the-oddysey-from-vietnam-to-america-an-interview
-with-van-anh-vo/.

12. Regina Carter: Call and Response

"This is ignorant": All quotes are from an author interview with Regina
Carter on July 20, 2021, unless otherwise noted.

"There were times": Andrew Lindemann Malone, "Regina Carter: Regina's
Reverie," *Jazz Times*, updated May 9, 2019, https://jazztimes.com
/features/profiles/regina-carter-reginas-reverie/.

"Even without amplification": A. G. Basoli, "ARTS ABROAD; Paganini's
Violin Encounters Jazz; Both Are Doing Well," *New York Times*,
January 2, 2002, https://www.nytimes.com/2002/01/02/arts/arts
-abroad-paganini-s-violin-encounters-jazz-both-are-doing-well.html.

"When I went": Lindemann Malone, "Regina Carter."

"Breathe when": Christian Howes, "Regina Carter / Jazz Violinist: In Her
Own Words," *Creative Strings Podcast*, episode 32, August 19,
2018, https://christianhowes.com/2018/08/19/regina-carter-creative
-strings-podcast-ep-32/.

"an investment in": "About MacArthur Fellows Program," MacArthur Foundation official website, accessed December 1, 2021, https://www.macfound
.org/programs/fellows/strategy.

Watch the Reverse Thread: NPR Music, "Regina Carter: NPR Music Tiny Desk
Concert," YouTube, May 21, 2010, https://www.youtube.com/watch?v
=fAVEuYk5qiw.

"the majority of": Regina Carter, producer, "Regina Carter - The Making
of Southern Comfort," YouTube, Jan 10, 2014, https://www.youtube
.com/watch?v=nDO1SL-gj98&t=9s.

"strives to illuminate": "Swing States: Harmony in the Battleground," Regina
Carter official website, accessed December 1, 2021, https://www
.reginacarter.com.

"Music teaches us": UCLA Herb Albert School of Music, "2021 Commencement
Celebration—The UCLA Herb Alpert School of Music," YouTube,
June 11, 2021, https://www.youtube.com/watch?v=J15BCj_FeNw.

13. Nova Wav: Songwriting and Producing Duo

"Music really found me": All quotes are from an author interviews with Brittany "Chi" Coney and Denisia "Blu June" Andrews on November 3,
2021, and January 7, 2021, unless otherwise noted.

Notes

"You should just": Lisa Machac, "Nova Wav: Believing in Magic," *Tape Op*, issue 145, September/October 2021, https://tapeop.com/interviews/145/nova-wav/.

"I started concentrating": Machac, "Nova Wav."

"I love the": JT Tarpav, "Songwriter Denisia 'Blu June' Andrews Talks Working with Mariah Carey on 'The Elusive Chanteuse,'" *The Source*, June 8, 2014, https://thesource.com/2014/06/08/exclusive-songwriter-denisia-blu-june-andrews-talks-working-with-mariah-carey-on-the-elusive-chanteuse/.

"It's like you": Tarpav, "Songwriter Denisia 'Blu June' Andrews."

14. Maria Elisa Ayerbe: Engineering Latin Sound

"Welcome to A Tiny Audience": *A Tiny Audience*, season 2, episode 8, "Carlos Rivera," directed by Pascal Jaquelin, written by Maurice Keizer, aired April 16, 2021, on HBO Latino.

"outstanding performance as": News Release, "2019 Class of Leading Ladies of Entertainment," Latin Grammy Recording Academy, October 11, 2019.

"You know how": "Breaking the Barriers of Sound from Colombia," SoundGirls, accessed May 11, 2022, https://soundgirls.org/breaking-the-barriers-of-sound-from-colombia/.

"I was totally": All quotes are from an author interview with Maria Elisa Ayerbe on May 25, 2021, unless otherwise noted.

"One thing I'm": Produce Like a Pro, "World Class 'Latin Pop' Engineer and Mixer: Maria Elisa Ayerbe," YouTube, January 29, 2021, https://www.youtube.com/watch?v=XQZ_KwgnBh8.

"A reggaeton track": Larry Crane, "Maria Elisa Ayerbe: 'You've Got to Tell Your Story,'" *Tape Op*, issue 135, February/March 2020, https://tapeop.com/interviews/135/maria-elisa-ayerbe/.

"If we don't": Crane, "Maria Elisa Ayerbe."

15. Sylvia Massy: Adventure Recording

"We need the sound": Sylvia Massy, "Microphone 'Boom' with Sylvia Massy and Tannerite," YouTube, February 18, 2019, https://www.youtube.com/watch?v=27bdv3MJch0.

"It sounded just": Eyal Levi, "Sylvia Massy," URM Podcast, episode 294, November 24, 2020, https://www.urmpodcast.com/ep-294-sylvia-massy/.

Notes

"friendly music": All quotes are from an author interview with Sylvia Massy on November 2, 2021, unless otherwise noted.

"how a song": Levi, "Sylvia Massy."

"We didn't have": Maxwell Strachan, "What It Was Like to Be a Woman and Work with Prince," *Huff Post*, May 2, 2016, https://www.huff post.com/entry/prince-women-tamar-davis-sylvia-massy-susan -rogers_n_57237248e4b0f309baf09a21.

"There's Prince sitting": Strachan, "What It Was Like."

"He thought that was": Strachan, "What It Was Like."

"Music is emotion:" Sylvia Massy official website, accessed July 21, 2022, https://www.sylviamassy.com/.

"Sometimes I write": Berklee Online, "Sylvia Massy on Her Career in Music Production," *TakeNote*, January 25, 2021, https://online.berklee.edu /takenote/sylvia-massy-on-her-career-in-music-production/#:~: text=Known%20for%20her%20playful%20style,to%20Johnny%20 Cash%20and%20Tool.

"Let's say you're": Levi, "Sylvia Massy."

"We tried it": Levi, "Sylvia Massy."

"No one will": Marc Young, "Sylvia Massy," *Shure Signal Path*, episode 16, April 10, 2019, https://www.shure.com/en-US/performance-production /louder/shure-signal-path-podcast-sylvia-massy.

"That way, you'll": IZ Connected, "Sylvia Massy on Women in Audio Engineering, Music Producing and Mixing," YouTube, October 3, 2016, https://www.youtube.com/watch?v=4SHRZy7plio.

Tribute to Sophie Xeon

"It should be mind-blowing": Julius Pristauz, "SOPHIE," *Glamcult*, issue 129, 2018, https://www.glamcult.com/articles/sophie/.

"He had brilliant" through *"Music, I suppose"*: Thora Siemsen, "SOPHIE on Criticism, Collaborating and Childhood," *Lenny Letter*, July 16, 2018, https://www.lennyletter.com/story/sophie-interview.

"I filtered a lot" through *"We'll just sit"*: Ivan Guzman, "The Future Is Sexy," *Office*, September 21, 2018, http://officemagazine.net/interview/future-sexy.

"Being trans was something": Harrison Brocklehurst, "SOPHIE: An Icon Who Made Music a More Fearless Place." *MixMag*, January 30, 2021, https:// mixmag.net/feature/sophie-musician-icon-dj-interview-feature.

"The main feeling": Guzman, "The Future Is Sexy."

"Blow people's minds": Brocklehurst, "SOPHIE."